Extravagant LOVE

A Gospel Gift
for
Disarming
the Heart

• • •

Mary R.
Schramm

AUGSBURG Publishing House
Minneapolis

EXTRAVAGANT LOVE
A Gospel Gift for Disarming the Heart

Copyright © 1988 Augsburg Publishing House

Scripture quotations unless otherwise noted are from the Holy Bible: New International Version. Copyright 1978 by the New York International Bible Society. Used by permission of Zondervan Bible Publishers.

Scripture quotations identified RSV are from the Revised Standard Version of the Bible, copyright 1946, 1952, and 1971 by the Division of Christian Education of the National Council of Churches.

Illustrations: David Martin

The poem by Joseph Pintauro on pages 84-85 is from *To Believe in Man* (Harper and Row, 1970). Reprinted by permission of Curtis Brown Associates, copyright © 1970 Joseph Pintauro.

The text of "A Mighty Fortress Is Our God" on pp. 126-127 is © 1978 *Lutheran Book of Worship*.

Library of Congress Cataloging-in-Publication Data

Schramm, Mary.
    Extravagant love : a Gospel gift for disarming the heart / Mary R.
Schramm.
        p.   cm.
    ISBN 0-8066-2304-7
    1. Peace—Religious aspects—Christianity.   2. Community of St.
Martin.   3. Schramm, Mary.   I. Title.
    BT736.4.S38   1988
    241'.697—dc19   87-32082
                                                                      CIP

Manufactured in the U.S.A.   APH 10-2152

1   2   3   4   5   6   7   8   9   0   1   2   3   4   5   6   7   8   9

This book is dedicated to the members of the Community of St. Martin, who live with the uncertainties and contradictions of making peace in a world of violence. I am grateful to those who share the risk and the joy of taking the vow of nonviolence. Thank you for your help in writing this book and for holding me accountable as we struggle together to live out a gospel alternative to violence.

Protector of peace, enliven us with
    a sense of humor, songs, and
    dreams.
Give us courage to speak truth
    and boldness to follow where
    you lead.
Above all, keep us tender and gentle,
    gifted with extravagant love.

CONTENTS

1

IN THE FULLNESS OF TIME

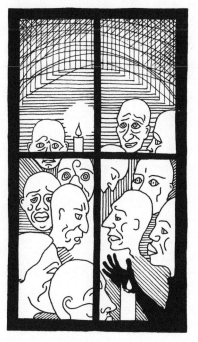

O nce upon a time—*kairos* time, the fullness of time for us and not necessarily the best time in our busy lives—came the moment we had agreed on to be together. It was dark outside, and the summer air was sticky. Inside the room we had drawn a dozen chairs together in a tight circle. We looked like settlers in covered wagons, finding a sense of security in our physical closeness. We didn't talk much. We sat quietly, waiting for everyone to arrive. The hour was late. We had come from other meetings, hospital duty that kept us overtime, or an early movie.

Anyone walking past the darkened building and looking in at us would have thought it strange to see 12 people sitting silently around some candles in various contemplative postures. They would have gone by shaking their heads, I suppose, calling us peculiar people.

The 12 of us were part of a worshiping group who for the previous two years had been trying to shape an intentional community, the Community of St. Martin. We had chosen the name because, as we looked at the history of the church there were many Martins who were models of peacemaking and nonviolent resistance:

Martin de Porres, Martin of Tours, Martin Niemoeller, Martin Luther King Jr.—and Martin Luther, for his theology of the cross.

At the center of our faith was a conviction that our vocation as Christians was to make connections between justice and peace. We needed the help of a supporting community to prod us into living out the connections we saw. Though our interests and values were similar, we were diverse in age and vocation—store clerks, a pastor, nurses, a peace activist, a teacher, a dramatist, an administrator, a psychologist. We were Roman Catholic, Lutheran, Greek Orthodox, and members of several other Protestant denominations. We were diverse, yet united in a desire to confess before God and before one another not only the violence within us, but also God's Spirit within.

For a year we had been examining a vow of nonviolence based on a vow written by Pax Christi USA. Pax Christi, the official international Roman Catholic movement for peace, was challenging Christians to reject explicitly the violence of this age, especially the violence associated with the arms race. To take the vow was to begin a journey toward disarming the heart. Tonight was the time we had set aside to begin our journey.

Some of our group were much farther along on the journey of responding to a world of violence with a mind and spirit centered on nonviolence. Nonviolent living had been part of their consciousness and lives for years. Nonviolence was an active, vital strength that sustained their day-to-day relationships. Others confessed they did not have nonviolence as the center of their spirituality, but they desired to understand how we disarm our own hearts as well as those of our enemies.

None of us thought it strange to take a vow. We had taken confirmation vows, and some had taken marriage vows. We were aware of the vows taken by those in religious orders. Ordination vows and the vows of elected public officials were not new to us. We did not struggle with the idea of a vow, but with its contents.

No one assumed that by taking a vow of nonviolence we had finally arrived at a life of love. We were convinced, however, that the vow could be a channel of grace, a way of opening ourselves to the work of the Spirit of peace within us. To take the vow was a way to say no to the apathy that trivialized strong convictions or paralyzed us with guilt and despair. It was a way to say yes to a new way of viewing enemies and those we dislike. It was a beginning attempt at reconciling ourselves to our sisters and brothers.

And so, we gathered on this night, at this *kairos* time, to share with one another our reasons for taking the vow. We listened and nodded our heads as we related to one another's struggles and concerns. Had we thought about it long enough? Would it be divisive in our worshiping community? What if some of us weren't really serious enough in our commitment to nonviolence? Was it a call on our lives or just a pressure to conform to other members of the community? What if we failed to live up to the vow? If we were truly nonviolent, would we be called to walk in paths that might lead to suffering or even death?

We had no illusions that we were somehow going to be better lovers than others in our faith community who were not taking the vow. We simply came together to express corporately the call of God's Spirit to be aware and awake—aware of our violent responses and awake to alternative possibilities. By taking the vow as individuals, and yet corporately as a community, we made ourselves accountable to one another. We were saying out loud what we felt in our hearts but had been afraid to trust only to our individual prayers and intentions.

Some of the candles had burned very low when we finally finished our prayers and our sharing. We stood up and together slowly read the vow:

> Recognizing the violence in my own heart and in the world around me, yet trusting in the goodness and mercy of God, I vow for one year to practice the nonviolence of Jesus who taught us in the Sermon on the Mount:
>> Blessed are the peacemakers, for they shall be called the children of God. . . . You have learned how it was said, "you must love your neighbor and hate your enemy," but I say to you, "love your enemies, and pray for those who persecute you. In this way you will be daughters and sons of your creator in heaven."
>
> Before God the Creator and the sanctifying Spirit, I vow to carry out in my life the love and example of Jesus
>> by persevering in nonviolence of heart;
>> by striving for peace within myself and seeking to be a peacemaker in my daily life through forgiveness and active, reconciling love;
>> by refusing to retaliate in the face of provocation and violence. Rather, I will seek creative responses to conflict;
>> by living conscientiously and simply so that I do not deprive others of the means to live;
>> by actively resisting the evils of oppressive structures and the causes of war;
>> by embracing the redemptive suffering of Jesus on the cross, accepting my own suffering which may result from active, nonviolent love, and being willing to enter into the suffering of others.

God, I trust in your sustaining love and believe that just as you gave me the grace and desire to offer this, so you will also bestow abundant grace to fulfill it.

The last part was a prayer and perhaps the most important aspect of the vow. It was not a statement of the strength we had as individuals or even as a community of faith. Instead, we were relying on the grace of God to live out this solemn promise we had made.

The vow challenged and stretched us, and we saw it as a source of growth in grace—an opportunity to deepen our relationship with God and with God's people.

2

Recognizing the violence in my own heart and in the world around me . . .

LET'S LIVE IN THE REAL WORLD

I have set before you life and death,
blessings and curses. Now choose life, so
that you and your children may
live....   Deuteronomy 30:19

Our world is violent. We do not need to look as far away as South Africa, the Middle East, Central America, or northern Ireland to point to examples of violence.

In the United States one of every four girls will be sexually assaulted before she is 18 years old, usually by a relative or family friend. One fourth of these abuses occur before the child is seven, and the abuse lasts from two to six years.

Nearly half the women murdered are victims of someone in their families. Twenty percent of all murders involve family relationships. (Statistics from "Families and Violence: The Church's Role" American Lutheran Church—Office of Church and Society document, 1986.)

I know a man who, whenever a crime has been committed in his area, is routinely picked up by police for questioning, simply because he is black. He has found it necessary to keep a record of his activities during the day to substantiate his whereabouts.

One hundred years ago males in this country were denied the legal right to beat their wives, and yet shelters for battered women are overflowing. A pastor friend who counsels wife abusers says the therapy groups in his rural Midwest community have long waiting lists of men whose choice is jail or prolonged counseling.

If women do manage to escape family violence, they often find themselves and their children facing the violence of poverty or a welfare system that continues to dehumanize.

Men are also victims, abused by their spouses verbally, psychologically, and sometimes physically. Manipulative anger, threats, and belittling are powerful tools of violence.

A small town in the Appalachian Mountains has one industry that employs a large percentage of the people in the county. The wages are low, and benefits limited. When the employees tried to unionize, the company threatened to move the factory out of the county. The employees, fearing loss of the few available jobs, felt helpless and gave in to the demands of the company. This is a form of violence against these people.

Violence can be subtle or overt. Educational systems that teach children and adults to pass tests but not to think, economic systems that allow wealth to be accumulated by fewer and fewer people, the unjust taking of land from its owners, medical care that caters to the wealthy, theological institutions that discriminate against some individuals—these are a few examples of how violence is woven into the fabric of our society. It seems difficult, indeed, to disarm the hardened hearts not only of individuals but of the institutions and the principalities and powers that control our lives.

The problem's too big!

At times I catch a glimpse of truth and of loving possibilities, but most of the time I feel inadequate to be anything other than my old judgmental, unloving self. I can't change the world. I can't even change me. The violence within *me* is a glaring reminder of how far I am from disarming my own heart or the hearts of others. I use this admission and my other inadequacies as a reason for apathy, as a rationalization for noninvolvement. I cling pathetically to my old ways of relating to family, friends, and even people I just don't like.

I rationalize that before I can start to be a model of love, my love must be perfect—and since it isn't, why try? Or I convince myself that the love of Jesus and his way of life is not applicable as a model in this age of violence. I tell myself there is nothing I can do. Evil is too overwhelming. The kingdom of God is seldom evident, and so I feel hopeless.

The Christian church teaches that in the person of Jesus, God established a new order of right relationships. Old patterns of relating were turned upside down (or rightside up). Enemies were to be prayed for, loved, and blessed. Those who took Christ's name were part of this revolutionary way of responding to all people.

But I misunderstand the nature of that kingdom and become confused. If the new kingdom is full of God-activity, it must be perfect, I say to myself. Perfect people will be involved, and the kingdom will be free of ambiguities, failures, and stressful living. The kingdom of God has gifted, respectful children, perfect parents, and coworkers who do not quibble or gossip. The kingdom of God has no grumpy postal clerks or people who cut in line. In the perfect kingdom government officials do not lie, and ad companies do not exaggerate. Everyone smiles and cooperates, shares, and gives generously of their time. People arrive on time, hangers don't get tangled, empty toilet-paper dispensers are refilled by the last person to use the bathroom, and no one leaves dirty dishes in the sink. Poems come easily, art is understandable, and sopranos don't have tremolos. No one has a disability, children are never hungry, everyone has a fulfilling job, and weapons are destroyed. Women celebrate the Eucharist, and men have good male confidants.

My childish view of God's perfect kingdom allows me the possibility of conditional living. Because perfection is not possible, I am relieved of the responsibility of even trying to disarm my heart of its anger and subtle hatred.

The disgusting neighbor will continue to mess up my sleep with loud parties and a noisy muffler. The mechanic will continue to charge me for parts I didn't need. My colleague at work will continue to take credit for what I do. And so I think, forget reconciliation until things are better! Forget working for disarmament or justice. I'll wait until I can be assured of results, wait until I am sure I won't get hurt or until I reap some personal benefit. I will wait until the rest of the world follows Jesus before I try to follow his example of nonviolent love of enemies.

Whether it is violence in personal relationships, hatred toward a neighbor, or the arms race, the problems seem beyond the scope of my ability to solve. One small voice will do no good, I think, forgetting that Jesus left the world in the hands of 12 rather slow-to-learn disciples. It may be that one small act of love will tip the balance.

We're all we've got

A time will come when we can expect God's kingdom to be perfect, but right now the kingdom is messy and full of inconsistencies. The realm of God is where God is working—here and now, in this place, with these people, with the economics of our modern world, in the theological struggles of a divided church, and with the ambiguities of contemporary ethics and morality. In a perfect world God's work would not be necessary, and we as God's disciples would be given the option of early retirement.

Because there are no perfect people in God's world, and because God has chosen us imperfect vessels to be bearers of the good news of God's unconditional love, we are without excuse. There is no one else assigned to reconciliation. There is no one else to love the unlovable. And so we get up each day and try to live faithfully, knowing that even when we fail to be forgiving and reconciling, God continues to forgive and reconcile *us*.

Part of our human condition is that we more quickly recognize the violence around us than the violence within. It is easy to make excuses for our complacency in regard to reconciliation or our complicity in the world's violence. Responding to violence in love calls for disarming the heart. The truth that God forgives and reconciles us should give us courage to drop our heart's defenses and lay down our weapons against those whom we call enemies. We are called to use other weapons—Spirit weapons of patience and joy, humility and gentleness—but, above all, extravagant love.

3

*Before God the Creator and the
sanctifying Spirit, I vow to carry out in
my life the love and example of Jesus . . .*

JESUS THE MODEL OF LOVE

*His only wealth was love and he spent
his fortune extravagantly; always and
everywhere.*   e. e. cummings

I wonder how I dared to "vow to carry out in my life the love and example of Jesus." The words stick in my throat as I realize how little my life exemplifies God-like love. I despair at the violence in our world, but even more devastating is the knowledge that not even my own life is a model of love.

The more I read the New Testament, the clearer it becomes that the life and love of Jesus were consistent with what he taught and preached. His life was centered in unconditional love for all people—disciples as well as enemies. He did not speak a better line than he lived. This makes it difficult for us to align ourselves with Jesus, because his *life* is the model, not his words.

If I want a way out of a radical following of Jesus, I listen to a small but sometimes loud voice within that asks if the violence we encounter today is similar to the violence in the world of Jesus. Perhaps in our world we can't be expected to embrace nonviolence.

Nothing much has changed

Our world is violent, but the world was also violent at the time of Jesus. The heavy hand of an oppressive government was almost intolerable for the Jewish people. There was no middle class. Poverty was rampant. Taxation was an unbearable burden for most. Women had no rights. Weaker nations were consumed by the powerful.

Jesus entered this world of chaos and violence and began to teach and to live an alternative way of responding to evil and oppressive systems.

If he were pastor of our church, we might consider him an embarrassment. He would not do well at attracting the wealthy, who could carry the financial burden of the next building program. He would not seem concerned with the gossip that surrounded his visiting with prostitutes or his eating with those unscrupulous tax collectors. His Sunday sermons would encourage us to live on half our income and share the rest with those unemployed steel workers who hang around the neighborhood bar. Those outcasts with leprosy and AIDS would get as much attention from him as the government official whose little daughter was dying. He'd even suggest that we need only one coat. During the prayers at worship he'd probably ask God to bless the Soviet people.

No doubt he would refuse to clench his fist and stand up like a man to those who opposed him or threatened his job, or to the church council who would ask him to resign. Now, as then, he would be despised and rejected; he would experience loneliness and deep grief.

Jesus and his fellow Jews felt the repression of a cruel Roman government and must have seriously considered violent revolution. The Zealot cause was attractive, and yet Jesus chose another way of relating to enemies. Hung on a cross as punishment for upsetting the social system, he continued to pray for his enemies and

refused to call down an army of angels as his personal
S.W.A.T. team.

In the book *Feast of Life* (World Council of Churches,
1982), John Poulton quotes a woman from the Federal
Republic of Germany, who compared the life of Jesus to
the militarism of today.

> Jesus lived without protection. That is not a statement of
> faith, just a plain observation. He renounced the protec-
> tion afforded by property. He did not use the protection
> of rhetoric but remained silent. He expressly rejected the
> protection of weapons and armies. . . . God has no desire
> to keep protected and unapproachable. God practices no
> violence. God has disarmed himself in Jesus Christ. Uni-
> laterally.

A woman at a workshop on nonviolence angrily
responded that she felt it naive to think we can live in
such an evil world and follow the example of Jesus. One
certainly cannot run a government on a love principle,
she said.

She may be right, but I don't want to come to that
conclusion. Before we can suggest nonviolence as a national tenet, we first need to address violence with nonviolence where we have the most power—in our own
lives.

The cycle of violence

Quaker professor Mulford Sibley told a group his
reasons for his pacifist stance. The first comment after
his talk was, "Dr. Sibley, I cannot believe how naive you
Quakers are about the fact of evil in the world."

"Oh no," the speaker responded, "it's just the opposite. It isn't that we are not realistic about the evil in
the world. It is because we see evil so clearly that we
refuse to have any part of it as our response *to* it."

Evil responses entrap us in the destructive power

of evil. Violence causes more violence, escalating the cycle of hatred and destruction. History should be our teacher. How often people who are oppressed and treated unjustly finally pick up the brick and hurl it through the bank window or at a police car. Then the oppressors scream, "Violence!" and repress the oppressed even more. Eventually by violent means the oppressed gain control of their lives and often begin to oppress the oppressors. The cycle of violence continues.

The same is true in personal relationships. I am hurt, so I look for ways to get even. I hurt the other person, who then feels there was justification for hurting me. The response is to find further ways of inflicting pain on me.

There is a folk dance in which everyone is in a circle, and the dancers go round and round as the music goes faster and faster. At one point the lead dancer lets go of the hand of the person on her left and breaks the circle, leading the dancers through different configurations, in and out of uplifted arms.

I think of this dance when I think of the possibility of breaking the cycle of violence. At any point we have the opportunity and the responsibility to step out of that circle of violence. The escalation of violence can stop with us. The love and example of Jesus compel us to respond with compassion, even at the risk of suffering.

The Spirit within us

In an imperfect world, in an imperfect kingdom of God, we imperfect people who call ourselves the body of Christ vow to carry out in our lives the love and example of Jesus. We do not undertake loving, creative acts of nonviolence by ourselves. We work in partnership with the Spirit of God, who always seeks to overcome evil with good and to overcome hatred with love.

Can we trust that Spirit? How much can we trust the love of God to be active in the world—to be active through us? If we trust God with our souls (there is nothing we can do to earn our salvation), is it possible to trust God with our lives, refusing to resort to the evil of violence?

In my community of faith we struggle with this question. We have no problem with the concept of working for disarmament. We know that when we aim weapons at the Soviet Union, a country with millions of Christians, we are aiming the forces of destruction at our own body—the body of Christ. In theory we applaud the years of nonviolent struggle for freedom lived out by the Christians of Namibia. We support the message of peacemaking taught by pastors and priests in El Salvador.

However, when we come to the possibility of personal violence happening to us on the streets of our city, the idea of a nonviolent response seems like the last option we would choose. At best it would be a tactic to protect ourselves. At worst it would be a cowardly, fearful response to a potentially violent situation. As my friend Kathleen said, "We are told to love others as ourselves. How can one respond passively and have love and respect for yourself?"

You can't. But nonviolence is not passivity. Nonviolence, properly understood and lived out, has the potential for being the greatest strength in the world, because it is the power of God's love *acting through us*.

Our daughter Karen was deeply hurt by vicious words from two girls at her school. She was new to the school and was seen as different from the others who had grown up in the area. I found her one afternoon, lying on her bed and sobbing into her pillow. When she told me what had been said, I asked what her response had been. Between sobs she told me she had said nothing, but had turned away quickly and started to cry. Now she wanted only to avoid these girls.

Many times this is what adult women do also. It is the passive response girls and women had been taught to make. This passivity is *not* nonviolence. Nonviolence is not some combination of passivity, capitulation, or running away.

What Karen eventually did *was* a nonviolent response. With a maturity and understanding that went beyond her age, she realized what she needed to do was to make friends of her "enemies." She did not want bad feelings and unkind words to stand between her and the possibility of making two new friends. The next day she said, "I think I'll make some cookies and take them as a gift. Maybe they'd like to see our house and spend the night with me. We could have a slumber party."

Nonviolence is a powerful, life-affirming, loving force for reconciliation. Nonviolence is a way to disarm hearts, to diffuse violence, to make friends of enemies.

Loving responses to conflict do not, however, always change the adversary so that each story has a happy ending. Jesus loved and prayed for his enemies and still hung on a cross. Love does, however, always change us. When we allow fear and mistrust and feelings of revenge to control our lives, we become slaves and not free women and men. The time, energy, and scheming we waste on jealousy, angry feelings, and self-protection become a violence we do to ourselves. A disarmed heart is a free heart. The heaviness of vengeful feelings is gone.

How extravagant can love be? If we model our lives after the one we call Lord, we have an answer. It is not the same answer the world affirms or encourages. But we are not of the world, and we can't wait for the rest of the world to follow Jesus before we act. Our living and loving is not determined by how good or inconsiderate, friendly or disagreeable other people are. It's easier and more fun to love certain people, but Jesus asks us, "If you love those who love you, what credit is that to you? Even 'sinners' love those who love them. . . . But love your enemies . . ." (Luke 6:32,35).

Our response to any form of violence needs to be love, not because our enemies are lovable people, but because the God who loves us loves our enemies too and commands us to do the same. We may not be responsible for all the evil and violence in the world, but we are responsible for working to disarm the hearts of those who perpetuate hatred and violence.

"Before God the Creator and the sanctifying Spirit, I vow to carry out in my life the love and example of Jesus." This will not be easy or even always effective. It is, however, a faithful way to live, and God calls us to faithfulness. It is life giving for us and for those who violate us. It is a way we say, "God loves you." We dare not undermine that love by verbal or physical abuse or by neglecting justice. To love as Jesus loved is also the way we show respect for ourselves by refusing to engage in similar violence.

The temptation to return evil for evil is great. But God lives in us, and God's ways—though we don't always understand or agree with them—provide a pattern and model for our lives. God is working in and through us. Therefore we are without excuse. Our love can be as extravagant as the love of God.

4

By persevering in nonviolence of heart...

IF YOUR EYE IS FULL OF LIGHT

We do not see things as they are. We
see them as we are.   The Talmud

Nonviolence is not a tactic, a strategy, or a certain demeanor we assume. Gandhi said, "Nonviolence is not a garment to be put on and off at will. Its seat is in the heart, and it must be an inseparable part of our very being."

Extravagant love does not come easy for us. We do not wake up one day and suddenly find ourselves to be people who live with extravagant, nonviolent love. The problems at work still cause tension and arouse angry or violent feelings in us. Family arguments and harsh words that hurt us do not disappear because we put on a smile. We still clench our teeth and feel coiled like snakes ready to strike.

I asked a study group to respond to Paul's words from Col. 3:15: "Let the peace of Christ rule in your hearts, since as members of one body you are called to peace." The responses were honest and sometimes hard for people to admit.

"I want this to be my experience, because I believe we were called to exhibit the peace of Christ, but when my friend lied about me, I wanted to get even. Then I felt very guilty."

"When I think someone is following me down the street at night, my heart is not peaceful. My heart pounds, and my palms sweat. I am sure the person behind me is my enemy."

"When my boss unjustly refused to promote me, I was angry and felt anything but peace."

"I yell at drivers (from the safety of my car) if they are moving too slowly on the freeway or if they cut me off in traffic."

"When I see a woman in the supermarket slapping her unruly child, I want to slap her back."

"When my spouse makes me angry, I use the old silent treatment."

"If someone is getting more attention than I think they should, I am inclined to say unkind things behind her back."

"In the apartment upstairs a mother was screaming at her teenage daughter, telling her she is ugly, inept, lazy, and a whore. I was furious and wanted to run upstairs and tell her she's a rotten mother!"

"I feel hateful toward governments and those in authority who allow unjust policies to oppress others."

"I was sexually abused by my father. I will never feel anything but hatred toward him."

With so much violence within us, how do we begin to "persevere in nonviolence of heart"? We hear the expression, "He had a change of heart," but how does this happen? How does one acquire a new way of seeing so that we arrive at a new perspective?

Our viewpoint is very important. "The eye is the lamp of the body. If your eyes are good, your whole body will be full of light. But if your eyes are bad, your whole body will be full of darkness" (Matt. 6:22-23). What is in our heart will determine what we see and how we respond to others in conflict situations. We do not always see things as they are; we more often see them as *we* are.

If we have been raised with the idea that our ultimate goal in life is to succeed in our chosen vocation, we grow up looking at anyone who seems to be standing in the way of achieving that goal as an enemy to be outsmarted. If we have always lived in a small town, with like-minded people of the same color and ethnic background, we will tend to look with suspicion and fear at those whose color and ethnic background differs from ours. If a young man grows up seeing his father dominate his mother with verbal or physical abuse, he may decide to treat his wife in the same way. Our government tells us who our enemies are, and we assume they must be destroyed. It seems easier to do if we call them "gooks," "spiks," "krauts," or "commies." A woman who has been raped on the streets of a city will view with fear and suspicion any man who walks behind her at night.

Some of our fears are well founded. Others are unwarranted. But when we let fear rule our lives, our hearts become violent, and we cannot respond with love.

In the struggle for black civil rights, the scene outside the First Baptist Church of Montgomery stands as a vivid example of how we try to intimidate others. Mobs of angry whites, fearing integration and their black neighbors, surrounded the church, carrying weapons and shouting threats. Inside sat hundreds of black women and men listening to Dr. Martin Luther King Jr. tell them that the state marshals were not able to control the crowd and had not been able to disperse them or bring order. Over and over he said, "But we must not be afraid. God is not dead. We shall overcome."

Ridding ourselves of suspicion and fear is not some-thing we are asked to do on our own. God lives in our hearts, so we open ourselves up in absolute trust to this possibility. "I will give you a new heart and put a new spirit in you; I will remove from you your heart of stone and give you a heart of flesh" (Ezek. 36:26).

Letting go of stony hearts

Many things make it difficult for us to allow God's Spirit to give us hearts of flesh. For one thing, old ways are hard to give up. I have often wondered why Jesus asked the blind man who came to him to receive his sight, "What do you want me to do for you?" (Luke 18:41). Surely Jesus knew. What a foolish question. He wanted to see! Why else did he come to Jesus? But the question is profound and is one Jesus could ask us. Do we really want to see? Do we want our eyes to be full of light so that change is possible?

Even the saints had difficulty with this possibility. St. Augustine in his famous line, "Make me pure, Lord, but not now," typifies our hesitancy to make a complete break with past attitudes and responses. We may have to swallow our pride or give up our old comfortable clothes of righteous indignation. Often it is more fun to sulk or to sit in a corner, licking our wounds.

It is difficult to let go of our anger. We cling to angry feelings like an old security blanket, because we feel comforted in our self-righteousness. As long as I am angry, I am right and you are wrong. Giving up a stony heart does not eliminate angry feelings, but it does mean confronting the anger in a healthy way. When our anger is acknowledged, talked about, and finally forgotten, relationships are strengthened. Saying nothing cannot bring reconciliation. As Thomas Mann wrote, "A word—even the most contradictory word—preserves contact. It is silence which isolates."

Recently a friend called to say how I had hurt him. He said he had felt put off, dismissed by my words and my attitude toward him. I was glad he called. I had been wrong and needed to be forgiven. Had he not called to express his anger, the foundation would have been laid for a wall that could easily have separated us.

There are many situations in which injustice and wrongdoing should evoke anger from us. Living non-violently includes relentless work against injustice, because where there is no justice, there can be no peace. But peace is not accomplished by unresolved, unrelenting anger. "I was so angry I could hardly see straight," is not just a cliché, but a fact. It is difficult to see clearly through angry eyes. Angry eyes may be unable to see anything but an avenue of revenge. Revenge hurts both parties. As Gandhi said, "An eye for an eye results in two blind persons."

In her book, *Brother Mouky and the Falling Sun* (Harper and Row, 1980) Karen Whiteside helps children and adults understand the work of forgiveness. Mouky's mother had taught him that he was "to be angry but sin not." She said to Mouky, "Never let the sun go down on your anger" (Eph. 4:26). This worried Mouky because he was furious with his brother. "My brother been giving me a hard time. . . . I got a right to be angry," Mouky stormed.

Late that afternoon when he looked up in the sky, he noticed the sun beginning to set. He pleaded with a tall building to stop the sun from setting by letting it rest on the flat rooftop. Then he hoped the tree could catch the sun as he saw it resting in the branch. But the sun got away and went sliding into the river, where Mouky watched it dancing. The river responded to his plea for help the same as the building and the tree. "Sorry, Sonny, sorry, sang the river slowly, without words. Sun, he have his job to do and I have mine . . . and now, you have yours, too."

Mouky hears the willow beside the river whispering, "Go home. Tell your brother his words hurt you. Let him say he sorry, and tell him it's okay. Tell him you forgive him."

Mouky had his work to do. He was to be reconciled to his brother. The anger he carried around all day was a heavy burden. The day was ending, and Mouky needed to disarm his own heart and initiate the sharing and listening, the forgiveness and love that brought him back into the family again.

The mind of Christ, the body of Christ

Writing to the church at Corinth, Paul said that we "have the mind of Christ" (1 Cor. 2:16). This Holy Spirit mystery within us began with our Baptism. Water and the sign of the cross on our foreheads signaled a new kind of life. We became part of a reconciling, forgiving family of God. This family isn't perfect, but it's all we've got. In the context of this family of God we have a chance to see and think and live the way Jesus did. Disarming our hearts, freeing ourselves from anger and violence, and moving toward disarming the hearts of others happens in the context of the people of God.

Forgiveness and transformation of violent situations can happen when those who love and support us help us to face the darkness in our souls and model for us eyes that are full of light. This always takes a conversion experience. God's Spirit enables us to let go of the violence and anger that imprison us. With a change of heart and eyes full of the light of Christ, we can make that peace of God, that mind of Christ, visible to the world. This peace which passes our understanding manifests itself in forgiveness, reconciliation, and justice. "Your attitude should be the same as that of Christ Jesus," is Paul's gentle suggestion for our own peace of mind (Phil. 2:5). Our minds are to center on concern for others.

In March 1987 Pastor T. Simon Farisani was again released from prison. It was only a few months before that this Lutheran Christian from South Africa was in the United States sharing the story of the persecution of the blacks in South Africa. I heard him speak of his other imprisonments by the government and of the torture he endured. As best as I can recall his story, this is what he said.

> People asked me how I found my courage during my imprisonment and torture. I am always embarrassed by that question. I was not courageous. Every time my torturers came near, I trembled and my knees shook. I was not strong. I prayed to God that I would die. I prayed to be relieved of the pain and anguish.
>
> One day I began to pray differently. I began with prayers for those who were torturing me. I prayed for as long as was necessary until each of those men was remembered before God. Then I prayed for those who had betrayed me, for the government officials who had sentenced me to prison for being a Christian. Then I prayed for others in the struggle for freedom in South Africa, for my friends and family. Only if there was time left did I pray for myself.
>
> I was overwhelmed by what happened to me. I strongly sensed that Christ was present with me in my cell. I learned that what Jesus said was right—God's strength was sufficient for me. I was flooded with a sense of peace

and a forgiving spirit. I had only to do what Jesus asked us to do—pray for those who persecute us, love those who are our enemies.

I feel very humble when I think of Pastor Farisani and grateful to God that we are both members of the family of God. I doubt that I could ever pass the test of faith as he did. I learned from his sharing that if we are to persevere in nonviolence of heart, we must keep before us the image of God in others. When we view others as enemies, our eye is full of darkness, and we fail to remember that they, too, are created with the capacity to love, to forgive, to create.

If we quickly say, "Oh yes, but these enemies are really awful people, they are terrible sinners," we need to remind one another that while *we were enemies* we were reconciled to God by the death of Jesus (Rom. 5:8, 10). All of us are God's enemies, reconciled to God. We will always have enemies. Our task is to be reconciled to one another as we are reconciled to God.

Pay attention

In *Death of a Salesman*, Willy Loman's wife pleads with her sons to change their attitude toward their father. "Attention must be paid!" she says.

Attention must be paid to those around us who are hurting and who have little self-esteem. Violence often occurs when individuals feel impotent and unable to take control of their own lives. To pick up a stone and hurl it through a window, to belittle another, to pull a knife, to beat a spouse, to badmouth a coworker, to rape—these actions come from a need deep inside. A child who rarely hears the words, "I love you," who has been ridiculed by classmates, who has seen 25,000 murders on television before he or she is 17 years old, who is never affirmed and applauded for achievements, will as a survival technique, have to prove himself or herself. Their anger and frustrations will be revealed in the statistics of street crime and spouse beating.

Pay attention, heart! Pay attention to the way we stereotype others. When someone of another race or culture, of another political persuasion or religious view approaches us, we instinctively put up an emotional wall of defense. We pre-judge. Our level of trust decreases. In our minds we make sweeping generalizations and quickly decide this person is stupid—or even evil.

A nurse friend of mine works with patients being prepared for surgery. Normally she doesn't work on Saturdays, but she had requested the following Monday off and was therefore assigned to work on the weekend. Monday was the day she was going to join in the protest action against a large company that manufactured trigger mechanisms for nuclear warheads. She had participated before in similar nonviolent protests and had spent time in jail because of her protests.

On this particular Saturday a man brought his wife into the hospital for emergency surgery. He was gentle with his wife and solicitous of her. The couple was nervous and preoccupied with the thought of the surgery. They kept calling my friend to stay with them. My friend is good at calming fears. She is sensitive and thoughtful and spent extra time with them. As she glanced at the woman's chart one last time, she suddenly realized the husband was the chairman of the large corporation that was the target of the protest on Monday.

"I couldn't believe it," she said as she told me the story. "I had the image of an uncaring, corporate executive who sat behind a desk, planning ways to fund and manufacture weapons of death. Instead I was confronted with a caring, compassionate man."

How often the protesters had wished for a meeting with this corporate executive! My friend began to wonder if it was professional for a nurse to discuss such issues as nuclear disarmament with someone in this situation. Perhaps God had somehow provided an opportunity for dialog.

After the wife was wheeled into surgery, my friend decided to tell the husband why she happened to be working on this particular day and where she was going to be on Monday morning.

The husband was dumbfounded. "You! You're one of them? I had the image of those people outside our corporation building being uncaring, strident radicals." She didn't fit his stereotype either.

The nurse and the corporate executive no doubt smiled as they were confronted with their stereotypes. They spent nearly an hour talking about the arms race and the corporation's participation in the manufacture of nuclear weapons.

I'd like to report that the company stopped making weapons and the world lived happily ever after. This is not the case. What did occur was a deeper understanding, a deeper trust, a new ability to view those we consider enemies as people also created in the image of God.

Seeing this God-image in others, letting go of our anger and our stereotypes, learning to forgive are first steps in persevering in nonviolence of heart. The Little Prince was right. "It is only with the heart that one sees rightly." It is what happens when God gives us hearts of flesh.

5

By striving for peace within myself...

CREATE IN ME A NEW HEART

> *Do not be anxious about anything, but in everything, by prayer and petition, with thanksgiving, present your requests to God. And the peace of God, which transcends all understanding, will guard your hearts and your minds in Christ Jesus.*   Philippians 4:6-7

Me worry? Of course, I worry. I'm anxious about many things. So are many other people. Among the most popular sections of any book store is the one with books offering suggestions on the difficult task of finding peace within.

There is a big market for "how to" books—how to live with failure, how to live with stress, how to stay in love, how to live almost happily with your teens, how to survive the loss of a loved one, or how to get yours when things around you are bad. Books offer counsel on how to make your marriage work, how to face a terminal illness, how to have a positive attitude, how to stay healthy, how to confront, how to forgive, and how to cope with just about anything.. The number of these books written and the number purchased, speaks to the universal anxiety pervasive in our society.

Our universal anxiety cannot be satisfied with the popular "peace of mind" quest. We need to redeem this phrase. Too often this quest for positive feelings and possibility thinking does not address the hard reality of injustice in the world. It forgets the risk of our involvement in the messy lives of hurting people. For many, peace of mind comes only when they are numbed to life around them. It is synonymous with tranquility and ends up being centered on self.

It is possible to have peace of mind by walking away from conflict or refusing to get involved. We can isolate ourselves as individuals, families, or congregations. We can avoid controversy by avoiding hard issues. Our family or congregation may, then, have peace of mind, but we will have forfeited the right to be called the body of Christ.

"Do not be anxious about anything." Paul's words to his beloved congregation at Philippi sound more like law than good news. When we're counseled not to worry, we think, "If I could stop worrying, I would!"

One evening at a shelter for the homeless, the evangelist gave his nightly sermon before his captive audience, the price hungry men had to pay for a meal. He ended his plea for morality and contentment by paraphrasing some lines from the Kipling poem "If." "If you can keep your head, when all about you are losing theirs and blaming it on you, then you will be a man, my son." The sermon was eloquent, but so was the response from the back row of the musty chapel: "And what if you can't?"

What if we can't? What if we can't find that peace within? Does striving for peace within belong in a vow of nonviolence?

Peace within is part of God's vision of wholeness for us. Interior peace is contagious. If, at the center of our being, we have allowed God's peace and the resulting freedom to possess us, others whose lives touch ours will have a better chance of finding their peace. Haven't we all been with people with whom we have immediately sensed a stilling of our own spirit? Their centeredness, the Spirit of God in control of their lives, shines in their eyes and is reflected in their care and concern for us and for a hurting world.

Say it out loud

Since I am not a psychologist or counselor, I will not pretend to have many helpful comments about the deep pain some of us must embrace if we are to discover a way for our spirits to be at rest. It does seem that part of finding that peace within is to acknowledge those times in our lives when we feel most distant from God, when God seems silent and aloof.

Children, for instance, fear nuclear war. In the small book *Please Save My World* (Bill Adler, Arbor House, 1984) children express their concerns. Billy writes, "I worry too much about nuclear war, and I'm too young to worry." Billy is seven.

Another seven-year-old comments, "Adam was the first man on earth. I hope I'm not the last."

Since Judith learned about the bomb she "doesn't smile much anymore."

Jessica, age 17, asks, "How are we supposed to start our lives with death looking over our shoulders?"

Anthony, who is in junior high, says, "It occurs to me that I may not grow up."

Children seem to have the ability to express openly many of their concerns. Adults are more hesitant. When God seems distant and unresponsive to our cries for help, for peace within, we can model the earthy, honest pleas of the psalmists.

Hear my prayer, O Lord; let my cry for help come to you. Do not hide your face from me when I am in distress. . . . I have become like a bird alone on a roof. All day long my enemies taunt me (Ps. 102:1, 7-8).

Or again:

> My God, my God, why have you forsaken me? Why are you so far from saving me, so far from the words of my groaning? O my God, I cry out by day, but you do not answer, by night, and am not silent (Ps. 22:1-2).

The words of Psalm 51 could be our prayer:

> Let me hear joy and gladness; let the bones you have crushed rejoice. Hide your face from my sins. . . . Create in me a pure heart, O God, and renew a steadfast spirit within me. Do not cast me from your presence. . . . Restore to me the joy of your salvation" (51:8-12).

These pray-ers were not afraid to say out loud what they felt in their hearts. There are as many reasons for our lack of peace within as there are individuals who seek answers as to where peace can be found. Sometimes the problem lies within us and is within our ability to solve. If we have been wrong, we need to say it out loud. If we need forgiveness, we have to ask for it. If we need help, we need to request it. If we have fears, they need to be expressed.

In everything present your requests to God, Paul wrote, but we also need to let those requests be made known to those closest to us. When we are lonely, hurt, afraid, or confused, we can risk sharing these human feelings with someone who cares about us. The very act of risking the emotion so close to our heart can begin to fill us with that elusive peace.

For many of us, growing up Christian meant growing up nice. We thought this meant that angry feelings are not nice and therefore not acceptable. But peace doesn't come when we deny those angry feelings. Gandhi said, "The acid test of nonviolence is that there is no rancor left behind, and in the end the enemy is converted to a friend." Rancor includes the unspoken, un-relenting angry feelings that churn inside our hearts.

Some have said that if pride is man's sin, passivity is woman's sin. Women have a difficult time overcoming the cultural assumption that womanliness does not include the expression of strong feelings. At a church conference, a woman in a leadership position stood up to make an impassioned speech about what she considered an injustice to women in the church. She spoke with some anger in her voice and with deep feeling. When the session was over, a bishop came up to her and admonished her for her outspokenness and anger. "It is not becoming for you to speak like this," he said. "You need to set an example for other women."

Some Christians think that confrontation and honest expressions of anger and pain are never acceptable. But where is there a better place to be vulnerable and verbalize our feelings than with those who share our faith values?

The violence we do to ourselves

We may be unwilling to confront one another and express our anger, but most of us freely express our lack of self-worth. We are very hard on ourselves. We dislike who we are and become self-destructive in our behavior by working too hard, many times at jobs that are not satisfying, or by overeating. We see only our weaknesses and tell ourselves critical things we would never say about others. Women, especially, assume that where there is a problem or a conflict, they are the ones at fault.

The passivity women often exhibit in response to conflict or anger from others comes from our feelings of inadequacy and worthlessness. Many women say things like these:

"My opinion doesn't really matter."

"They know more than I do, and what I might think doesn't matter."

"I'm tired of being ignored or put down, so I'll just keep quiet."

"What if someone finds out I'm shallow and not very smart?"

"I've failed before, so I won't try again."

So often we feel life is beyond our control, and our insecurities ooze out like spring sap from a tree. We question our abilities, our relationships, our past realities and future uncertainties. We say to ourselves: "Mozart was composing music when still in diapers. What have I done with my life?"

All of these thoughts deny our worth, our unique giftedness that makes us the person we are. We do not have to prove ourselves to God or to anyone else. Our worth has been established by a God who created us for a purpose, just the way we are. Our worth was vindicated by Jesus, who risked all in love to bring us back into a relationship with our Creator, and by the Spirit of God who lives within us. All we are asked to do is to *express* that worth and uniqueness.

Before his death Rabbi Zusya said, "When I die, they will not ask me 'Why were you not Moses?' They will ask, 'Why were you not Zusya?'"

The most peace-filled people I know are those who find ways to express their uniqueness and their giftedness. They understand their worth and connect their gifts to the needs of a global family.

I think we are so hard on ourselves because we do not understand grace. We are harder on ourselves than we are on others and certainly harder on ourselves than God is. We forgive others more quickly than we forgive ourselves. At times we are so immune to the good news of God's love that we scarcely allow it to affect us, and we miss another chance to be filled with God's peace. Sometimes the reality of this God-love washes over us when we least expect it.

The movie *The Great Sandini* is the story of a military family and the father who treats his children and wife as if they were under his command. As the story unfolded, I began to feel the resentment of the children as their father pushed them to be something other than who they were. He tried to strip them of their personhood and create them in his image.

The alienation between the father and children and between the husband and wife grew stronger until the desperate father became abusive. Realizing his condition and the gulf he had created, he ran out of the house, drunk and violent.

The children were crying and confused. The mother looked at her oldest son who had suffered the most from his father's expectations, and quietly said, "Go find your father. We must let him know that we love him."

The son ran through the dark streets of the town searching and calling, "Dad, where are you? We love you, dad." He found his father, stumbling through a park, broken in spirit, not realizing his need of forgiveness and love.

At first the father rejected the nonviolent love and outstretched arms of his son. He threw stones and swore and tried to run away into the darkness, but he could not escape his son's love. He finally allowed the son to hold him in his arms, a forgiven, loved, reconciled man.

Nothing we can do will cause God to take away from us the undeserved love and forgiveness that keeps calling us back when we run away, broken and hating ourselves. It is a love that gives us yet another chance to start again. This is grace. This is the peace of God that passes all human understanding.

Peace as *ping*

The Chinese word for peace is *ping*. *Ping* implies two ideas held in tension as symbolized by the *yin-yang* circle. For the Chinese, peace comes when there is balance in our lives. A good speaker will feel some tension but must give the appearance of being very relaxed. In your body, muscles counteract one another to keep you standing or sitting upright. Psychiatrists talk about the "pain of health," and the family doctor says no matter how we hate to exercise, in order to stay healthy we need to discipline ourselves to do it. The Benedictine order was established with the idea of balance in life. Work, play, worship, study must be held in tension if we are to experience *ping*.

The vow of nonviolence begins with a promise to strive for peace within, because if we do not desire and embrace the possibility of interior peace, it is difficult to be a peacemaker with others. We rarely do anything inconsistent with the way we live out our individual lives.

We do not, however, have to wait with our peacemaking until we have found perfect peace within. Life is not perfect. It is full of inconsistencies and often is out of balance. We spread ourselves too thin, make too many commitments, and wonder why our stress level is so high. We discover that our frantic efforts at making peace are leaving us anything but peace filled.

I discover this most often when my inner feelings fail to line up with my outward actions. Peace Pilgrim, the woman who has walked thousands of miles to raise our awareness of peace, wrote: "To attain inner peace you must actually give your life, not just your possessions. When you at last give your life—bringing into alignment your beliefs and the way you live them—then, and only then, can you begin to find inner peace" (Compiled by Friends, Ocean Tree Books, 1983).

"In everything, by prayer and petition, with thanksgiving, present your requests to God," Paul wrote. Dag Hammarskjöld said it this way: "For all that has been, thanks. For all that will be, yes" (*Markings*, Ballantine, 1964). And then that peace of God, which we cannot understand, will invade our hearts and our minds. This is grace, a gracious gift from a gracious God. We can claim it as our own, because whether we are up or down, effective or ineffective, we are God's. Nothing can separate us from that love. In that love we find our deepest peace.

6

By seeking to be a peacemaker in my daily life through forgiveness and active, reconciling love . . .

AN AWESOME POWER TO CREATE OR DESTROY

Blessed are the peacemakers, for they
will be called [children] of God.
Matthew 5:9

We hold within our being an awesome power. I am not talking about technology that puts men and women into space, or manipulative force that controls others. This power is our ability to give or withhold life by giving love or refusing to give it.

Ethicist Beverly Harrison writes that "the awe-full, awe-some truth is that we have the power through acts of love or lovelessness literally to create one another." She says we do not understand "the depth of our power to thwart life and maim one another. The fateful choice is ours, either to set free the power of God's love in the world or to deprive each other of the very basis of personhood and community" ("The Power of Anger in the Work of Love: Christian Ethics for Women and Other Strangers," *Union Seminary Quarterly Review* XXXVI, 1981).

This is a bittersweet concept. It is both exhilarating and frightening to think of our lives in relationship to those closest to us and realize our potential for tearing down or evoking the goodness in them.

Nonviolence is active, reconciling love that begins in the everyday situations that make up life for us. Of all areas of life, nonviolence toward those whose lives daily touch ours is the most difficult. We didn't choose our relatives; they were a given. Often we don't choose those with whom we work. Our faith communities often seem to consist of those people we least like to be with. Most pastors would not choose the people who make up their congregations. For the most part we are stuck with those folks around us. We have the power to enliven or to destroy them.

The power of the tongue

The tongue is one of the most violent weapons we possess. Such a little thing, James wrote, and yet it is like a bridle in the mouth of a horse or the rudder of a ship. "Likewise the tongue is a small part of the body, but it makes great boasts. Consider what a great forest is set on fire by a small spark" (James 3:5).

Our tongues can curse others or praise God. They can incite to riot or calm fears. The words we speak can bring another to heights of joy or send them into the depth of despair. We can inspire our children to become creative, fulfilled individuals, or withhold any words of encouragement and watch as they become aggressive, unhappy adults.

If you think you are a person of faith and don't know how to bridle your tongue, James wrote, you deceive your heart, and your religion is vain. Strong words to his readers and strong words to us who thrive on our ability to use words and words and more words.

If only we could take back some of the things we have said! As soon as the words are out of our mouth, we wish we had swallowed them or wish we could catch them before they fly off into the wind. Martin Luther once challenged a woman to retrieve her words of gossip. It is, he said, like trying to retrieve feathers from a pillow being blown by the wind. It is impossible to stop the words or to undo the damage of idle or malicious gossip.

A pastor found a good way to squelch gossip that came to him. As soon as someone would say, "Did you know . . . ?" in that smug, secretive way we have of imparting knowledge, he would quickly get out his little red appointment book and say, "Now let me get this straight—the date, your name, the particulars." He has yet to make an entry in his book.

Our tongues are weapons when the things we say alienate one person from another or when our words are intended to discredit, hurt, or bring revenge. When I took the vow of nonviolence, I found it important to list the specific areas of concern for me in the use of my tongue. Your list may be different but these are things I need to remember:

I will not share things said in confidence to me.

I will not say anything about someone else that I am not first willing to share with them personally.

Am I attempting to build up my own ego by criticizing another?

Is what I say about others said in love, and is it a way to build up their self-esteem?

If I am angry, I will wait until I have thought about the incident before I confront the other person, lest I blow the episode out of proportion.

These are simple, obvious reminders, but it is in these areas that many of us stumble in our daily peace-making. James would write to us today, "Know this, people that I love, be quick to listen and slow to speak in anger, for words spoken in order to hurt another are not what God has in mind for setting things right" (James 1:19-20 author's paraphrase).

The apostle Peter closely linked the use of our tongue with God's blessing:

> Never repay one wrong with another, or one abusive word with another; instead, repay with a blessing. That is what you are called to do, so that you inherit a blessing. For who among you delights in life, longs for time to enjoy prosperity? Guard your tongue from evil, your lips from any breath of deceit. Turn away from evil and do good, seek peace and pursue it. For the eyes of the Lord are on the upright, his ear turned to their cry. But the Lord's face is set against those who do evil.
>
> (1 Peter 3:9-12 New Jerusalem Bible)

The power of forgiveness

Judy works with me, and I treasure her friendship and her insights. Not long ago her father died. He had been ill for 20 years with a heart condition. The doctors were perplexed as to why he was still alive. He seemed to cling to his life in spite of its poor quality.

The relationship between Judy and her father was not good. As a child she had loved him deeply. He was everything a father could be and the only dad on the block all the kids called by his first name. As she grew to adulthood, the relationship for some reason had soured. She began to think of him as her tormentor, her adversary. He no longer hugged her hello or said "I'll miss you" when she left. The estrangement had been long and painful for my friend. She never understood what happened to the love between them.

One summer day Judy traveled to see her father. Other friends of her dad were there, and the week's visit did not go well. It was difficult to see all the old patterns unchanged, to hear the same criticisms, and to try to get past his cold, distant, unloving attitude.

In frustration and anger Judy left for her home. "I had been driving for about an hour," she said, "when I realized there was another presence with me in the car. I had been crying so hard I scarcely noticed, but I sensed someone—something—saying to me, 'Stop the car and call your father.'

"I can't explain it, but I literally did battle with that presence. I felt anger and deep pain, and the last thing I wanted to do was to call my father and speak with him again. I argued with the presence and defended my position."

Then Judy began to think of the good things that had happened between them in the past. She remembered the time when she had loved him deeply, when he had been a wonderful father to her.

"I lost the battle," she said. "I saw a phone booth at a roadside park and stopped the car and called my dad. I asked that his best friend get on the extension phone so he could hear what I was saying to my father and substantiate my words."

She began to tell him how she remembered the good times and that much of what people liked and admired about her were things she had learned from him.

"Big deal," came his response. "So why are you calling me now?"

"To tell you that the gifts you gave to me can never be taken away from me," Judy replied. "The gifts you gave me are what I share with others. I will always be grateful for them."

His response? "I don't like you, and I wish we could be separated. There is nothing between us anymore."

"You're right," she sadly concluded, "but I just wanted to tell you these things."

"Thanks for nothing," was the last thing Judy heard her father say.

Several weeks later he died. "I really feel that what I said released him to die," Judy told me. It also released her to live. Having lost the battle with the "presence," she gained the freedom and peace that is the result of extravagant, nonviolent love.

The power of abandonment

"I'm right, and you know it!"

"You hurt me, so admit it."

"I was here first."

"I deserve it more than you."

"You should be the one to apologize."

Sound familiar? To be a peacemaker sometimes takes no more than to abandon our "rights," and graciously and humbly be the first to say a quiet word of forgiveness or say, "I'm sorry."

This is hard to do. We are not taught to give up rights and privileges. Our courts are full of people demanding their rights. The legal system has an overload of cries for "justice." Whenever possible, people yell "Whiplash!" "Grab what is yours, and make the other person pay until it hurts" is the motto. "I'll see you in court," is getting to be a common way to say good-bye.

Writing in *The Reconciler*, a publication of the Christian Conciliation Service, Lynn Buzzard says, "The courts are not only overloaded by a surge of litigation, but are ill-equipped to provide relief from the tensions, losses, and frustrations which pervade modern society. . . . It is precisely in the extremes of intimacy and anger that much conflict today resides—in families, in small communities, in churches, and between partners. The courts can neither grasp nor effectively address these deeply personal, emotional elements of human behavior."

We have legal systems because we haven't learned to relate to one another in love. We need our courts, because of human greed and brokenness, but they are not an easy fix for resolving conflict. Rarely are two parties reconciled as a result of legal action.

As peacemakers, we have power in conflicts that arise between the extremes of intimacy and anger to "win a brother over," as Jesus says, or the power to further alienate our adversary. Most of us are selective in regard to Scripture, and we have chosen to ignore ways of resolving conflict that Jesus taught.

> If your brother sins against you, go and show him his fault, just between the two of you. If he listens to you, you have won your brother over (Matt. 18:15-16).

Then, Jesus says, if he doesn't listen, take one or two others along with you as witnesses to what you say. If there is still no resolution of the conflict, tell it to the church. It is in this context that Jesus says, "Where two or three come together in my name, there am I with them" (Matt. 18:20).

At another time, Jesus said, if you have gone to worship and suddenly you realize that someone has something against you, go and make amends with that person (Matt. 5:23-24). Go the extra mile. Be creative in your responses to conflict.

Sometimes our peacemaking will be to guide others into peaceful and creative ways of resolving conflict.

In the mountains of West Virginia the only surveyor in one remote county is our friend Tom. He once helped mediate a dispute between a brother and sister who were trying to decide on a division line between his mobile home trailer and her shack. They were not receptive to his proposal as surveyor so he left them alone to try to decide on a line. Six months passed and a complete impasse was reached; they were not speaking to each other, their children were fighting, and tension was evident on every side. He proposed mediation at that point and described the process to them. They did not like the idea but figured it was worth a try since they had to get the property divided in order to get title to their respective properties and be able to get a loan to fix up their property.

A meeting was arranged in the basement of the nearby Presbyterian church. A friend who had taken a mediation course with Tom joined him in conducting the session. First, they explained the procedure and guidelines and let each party tell their story uninterrupted. Then they drew from them their thoughts on how the land might be divided. The brother volunteered that he would accept equal acreage if his sister would. She agreed, and in his capacity as land surveyor Tom said he could achieve that. Then they grappled with the tough question of where the division line should be between their dwellings that were less than 40 feet apart. The brother said he was worried because eight feet of his mobile home trailer was on Forest Service land and the Forest Service might make him move. Then Tom proposed a division line splitting the distance between the two dwellings after allowing eight feet extra for the brother's trailer. This proposal was accepted by both parties and, with plenty of equal acreage, became the basis for settling the dispute and eventually for healing the friction between brother and sister.

For the sake of others, Jesus did not think his rights a thing to be grasped (Phil. 2:6). For the sake of other followers of Jesus will choose to let humility and a sense of abandonment replace "me" and "mine." It is in our everyday relationships that this theological truth is put into practice. It is not easy to overcome hostility with love. Lashing out in retaliation seems easier. We have to learn to make peace, just as we have been taught to make war.

Recently, when we were with friends in Seattle, we were reminded of their continuing struggle for reconciliation with some neighbors. Our friends have a dog that once badly injured the neighbor's dog. Our friends were taken to court even though they agreed to pay for any medical treatment. The judge put them on probation and told them to keep their dog locked in a pen.

Unfortunately, some time later, a dog that closely resembled the animal belonging to our friends roamed through the neighborhood. Thinking our friends had broken their probation, the neighbors called the police to report that the dog was not penned. Even when the neighbors discovered this was not the case, they did not apologize. The stray dog continued to prowl around, and the neighbors continued to call the police.

For nearly a year our friends responded with gentleness to the angry neighbors. "We made it a point to talk with them whenever we saw them in their yard," Ellen told us. "We called them when we saw the stray dog and assured them our pet was in the pen. I made cherry pies and coffee cakes as peace offerings, but mostly we prayed about the situation." Ellen wasn't sure if it was the prayers or the cherry pie, but there was and is a softening in the hostile attitude of the neighbors.

There is power in letting go of "I'm right," or "Me first," or "You're wrong." Neither Tom nor our Seattle friends feel like Gandhi or a Martin Luther King Jr. Yet their efforts at nonviolently disarming hearts witnesses to the awesome power of extravagant love.

The power of example

Any discussion of nonviolence in daily life should include a look at how we raise our children. It is in the family that our children are trained for life in society. Parenting involves more than feeding, clothing, and educating those in our care. We are also responsible for teaching them how to relate in love to those around them.

Our children will become part of communities in which gospel values are not the norm. They will grow into a world where "might makes right" and where winning is everything. The culture will reinforce individualism by dictating that it is most important to take care of number one. Independence will take precedence over interdependence. Our children will learn that we should go to any length to protect the "good life" to which we have grown accustomed.

Alternative ways of living and relating need to be taught from the time our children are born. They will learn by our example. Ivan Illich wrote:

> We can only *live* changes. We cannot think our way to a new humanity. Everyone of us, every group with which we work must become a model of the new era we hope to create. The many models which will develop should give each of us an environment in which we can celebrate our potential and discover the way to a more humane world.

Begin with a commitment to caring. One of the reasons our children are sensitive to the needs of others is that they had a grandmother who was never too busy to take the time to care about those little things that trouble children. A shoelace to be unknotted, a story that "had to be read," a button that had popped off, a childish conversation that was important to them—all these were attended to quickly and with loving concern.

Children who learn peacemaking at an early age generally are around adults who care about the suffering of others. A couple we know took their teenage sons to California for several summers so they could work beside migrant workers and learn what it is to eke out a living in a strange land. These children have learned that "to pray without ceasing" is to carry the anguish and pain of the world always in their hearts.

All of us are parents, aunts, uncles, teachers, friends, or grandparents of children. We hold an awesome power to create one another. Children will learn nonviolent, peacemaking skills by watching us. They observe how we spend our money, what takes priority in our time commitments, and how we resolve conflicts. They listen to what we say about others. They hear us discussing our charitable giving and our income-tax returns. They sense our attitudes about those of another race or culture, how we feel about street people or the woman in the grocery line with food stamps in her hand. They know where we put our trust, the depth of our faith, our level of self-esteem, and if we are truthful. If we are indulgent, lack consistency in our discipline, or place no limits on them, they will become confused and anxious. If we admit our mistakes, they will hear.

Peacemaking is habit-forming. It first takes a decision to live nonviolently and then a commitment to live out that decision. Forgive one another. When you have forgiven seventy times seven, forgive again. Negotiate. When you have talked and talked, talk again. Those who make peace will be called the children of God.

7

By refusing to retaliate in the face of provocation and violence. Rather, I will seek creative responses to conflict . . .

LOVE DOES MORE THAN CONQUER

*Against the ruin of the world, there is
only one defense—the creative
act.*   Kenneth Rexroth

Conflict situations arouse the best or the worst in us. When someone is trying to cheat, hurt, or frighten us, or defame our character, we respond from the core of our being. That core—our faith, what we value—will be reflected in our outward response. Gandhi had a word for this "soul power" within us. He called it *satyagraha* which means "holding to truth." A disarmed heart will respond very differently from a heart seeking revenge or protection.

This is not a new discovery. In the letter of James we read:

> Can both fresh water and salt water flow from the same spring? My brothers, can a fig tree bear olives, or a grapevine bear figs? Neither can a salt spring produce fresh water. . . . Peacemakers who sow in peace raise a harvest of righteousness (3:11-12, 18).

James is trying to make it clear that we cannot be who we are not. If we have a jealous heart and try to fake a loving response, or try to respond nonviolently when we have violence inside, not only will our response be shallow and suspect, but there will be a tearing of our spirit as we try to bring forth pure water from a brackish spring. This is why the vow of nonviolence began with promising to be a peacemaker by persevering in nonviolence of heart.

We learn to make peace

In the vow of nonviolence we promise to use creative responses to conflict rather than initiate or participate in retaliation. Creative responses are learned. We learn to make peace. We begin by asking ourselves what we desire to have happen in any conflict situation. Is our goal to humiliate the assailant or the enemy? Do we want to injure, maim, or kill our opponent? Is the bottom line that we protect ourselves regardless of what we do to our adversary? Perhaps we wish to dominate, control, or manipulate. We should be very clear about our intention, because this will determine our response. If we have been trained only in violent ways of responding, we have little chance of finding resources inside us for creative resolution of the problem.

In his book *What Would You Do?* John Howard Yoder lists many ways of relating to an adversary. He wrote the book because, like most pacifists, he is always asked the question, "But what if someone came into your house and tried to harm your baby, rape your grandmother, or assault your wife?" While these things rarely happen, they are the first questions people ask if they want to discredit a pacifist view of responding to violence. Many genuinely do not see nonviolence as an effective, or even a faithful, response of Christian discipleship.

What *does* one do? Our response will be determined by how we view human life—ours and that of our opponent; by the amount of trust and faith we have in a

God of history; by our desire to witness to the adversary about the love of God; by our respect for the humanity and the God-image of the other person; by whether we consider our life or that of a family member, neighbor, or countryman of more value than that of the enemy. These certainly are not all the determining factors, but they are a start. Perhaps a true story will help illustrate what I am trying to say.

Maggie lives on the near north side of Minneapolis. As big cities go, this is not a dangerous neighborhood, but it is one of the high-crime areas of Minneapolis. Early one autumn evening Maggie was out running. She had run farther than she had planned, and it was getting dark as she headed for home through a secluded wooded area.

As she turned a corner, she was accosted by a large man, who grabbed her and tried to pull her off the path. "Come on, we're going this way," he said as he dragged her by the arm and pinned her against a tree.

Maggie was tired, angry, and frightened. She remembered thinking three things. First, that his eyes looked very wild as if he were on some kind of drug. Second, that she was home alone this weekend; no one would miss her until Sunday evening. And third, that she was so frightened she felt completely immobilized.

"By the grace of God, along came a man with his dog," Maggie recalled. "I saw him through the dark and realized he was a very small man. I thought to call out for help, but I became concerned that because he was so small, he might also be hurt."

By this time, her assailant released some of the pressure from her shoulders and became very anxious. Concerned for the safety of all three of them, Maggie took the assailant's arm as he had taken hers and used his words. "Come on, we're going this way."

She led him in the opposite direction from the man and his dog. The assailant looked at her in disbelief and said in amazement, "Why did you do that?"

Maggie looked at him and said gently, "I can tell by the look in your eyes that you've experienced a great deal of hurt. Perhaps it would be better for us to talk than to do whatever it was you had planned."

They had reached the Plymouth Avenue bridge that went over the path, and Maggie gently sat him down on one of the bridge footings. She began to talk with him. She took the opportunity to remove herself from the role of victim by telling him about her family and her own life. She asked him if he had family and friends in Minneapolis.

The man had been a Marine in Vietnam, and his job was that of executioner in a small village. He had been responsible for lining up victims, including women and children, and shooting them. He talked about the experience, about his family, and the deep pain in his life. Maggie humanized him as much as possible and became a caring person to him by the way she listened and responded.

It was very dark by now, and Maggie, with her usual good humor, wasn't sure how to make a graceful exit. Had the encounter changed enough so that she was free to go? Does one say, "May I leave now?" or "What were you *really* going to do?" Instead she said, "It's dark now, and my husband will be worried about me. I don't like to walk these streets alone at night. Would you be willing to walk me home?" (She neglected to mention that her husband and three children were out of town for the weekend.) The man walked her home and said good night.

The next day Maggie found a bouquet of daisies inside the screen door with a note: "Thank you for being my friend. You listened to me."

Not all such stories have happy endings. Maggie could have been assaulted and raped. It happens often on the streets of our cities. The women in our faith community heard her story with a mixture of admiration and head shaking. What kind of resources did Maggie rely on? we wondered. Does it take training and a different kind of faith than most of us have? Was Maggie just naively dumb or a superwoman? We asked her several questions.

Why do you think he didn't rape you? Why didn't he run when he had a chance?

MAGGIE: I believe I really surprised him when I took his arm and was willing to stay with him. I tried to show concern for him. In his mind the scenario would include a physical struggle, panic, screaming. I took the struggle from the physical plane and moved it to the moral. I think this surprised and intrigued him. Studies show that one cannot be in a state of surprise and wonder and also in a state of aggression and violence. It is physiologically impossible. Even the use of humor can allow you the opportunity to take control of the encounter.

In assault situations victims usually have more moral and personal resources than they think they do. We need to use these resources. This is not to say we won't feel fear. We will! Just don't act out of that fear.

Why do people do these kinds of things?

MAGGIE: Most psychologists suggest that aggression is "the manifestation of human brokenness." In his book *Power and Innocence* (Norton, 1972) Rollo May says that every person goes through five stages of personal power.

In infancy the baby just is. The power to be is satisfied by responsive parenting. In early childhood, self-esteem and self-affirmation emerge. If these are blocked when the child is told he or she is stupid, no good, uncreative, the child will be driven to become a highly competitive person.

Later, personal power is revealed in self-assertion: "Here I am. You better notice me." If people still fail to notice or affirm that individual over a long period of time, the individual will seize power by aggressive behavior. We see this in race riots, for example, after long periods of exploitation.

The fifth level of personal power is the violent act. Violence in an individual is a sure sign that the assailant comes to us as a broken person. As Christians we have a choice. We can evoke that brokenness, or we can reach for the image of God in that person, expecting the person to do what is good and right.

Has it helped to study this?

MAGGIE: Obviously it helped me to understand that the person who may try to harm me has a history of rejection, pain, and conflict. It is difficult not to feel a deep sense of compassion for someone who has been deeply hurt. These are the very people Jesus came to be with—the hurting and the oppressed who found themselves rejected by society. Much of this I learned from the Pax Christi workshops on deterrence to personal assault.

How did you overcome fear and have so much courage?

MAGGIE: I think you are always afraid. But again, let me mention some thoughts from Rollo May's book. Courage is not the opposite of fear. Courage implies readiness to fight, to risk oneself, to match body and mind against the adversary. Soldiers are supposed to be courageous.

In contrast to courage, love involves not only willingness to risk, but moves conflict to a higher level. Love guides and manipulates, in the best sense of that word, because of its emotional energy. Love does more than conquer; it seeks to unite.

But you could have been killed! Don't you have a responsibility to protect yourself?

MAGGIE: But don't you see? I did protect myself, as well as protect the man who grabbed me. Had I tried to injure him or fight back, chances are we both would have been hurt. A nonviolent response creates a different kind of climate. If we refuse to fall into the trap of responding to aggression with violence, we have the possibility of changing the assailant's response. Striking back only reinforces his violent behavior and justifies his need to continue to be violent. Violent resistance limits the conflict at the level of conflict. In other words, you limit yourself to playing the game by the assailant's rules.

How can you love a person like that enough to respond nonviolently?

MAGGIE: If we can't love that person even a little, perhaps we can respect the fact that this is a *loved person.* God loves that person, and God loves me. This helps me approach the adversary differently.

I understand that love of God intellectually, but if I were being threatened, how could I treat that person as someone God loves deeply?

MAGGIE: We are all loved with the same love originating with the parent-God, and because of God's indiscriminate love, the assailant's safety is as important as my own safety. In the incident that happened to me, I was quickly aware that three people could have been hurt and that we all needed to make it through the encounter safely. To me, nonviolence is the manifestation of my commitment and participation in this kind of love.

If you knew you were going to die and had a knife, would you have used it?

MAGGIE: No. I'm ready to meet God. I could not be sure the other person was.

The result of this conversation with Maggie was a Women and Nonviolence support group that meets once a month. The group realized the importance of being spiritually and mentally prepared if we hope to meet conflict situations with nonviolence. We want to nurture the kind of faith and attitudes within us that allow for spontaneous, loving responses.

After this heavy conversation we found relief in laughter as Kathleen told us her story of being held up at gunpoint in New York City. "I was sure no Maggie. When I saw that gun, I was petrified. I became like a statue. I literally was not present to the situation in mind or spirit. I blocked it all out and can't even remember handing over my purse."

I'm sure that's how I would have responded. I would have been like the Essenes at the time of Jesus, who avoided conflict by fleeing to the desert. In threatening situations, if nonviolent resources and convictions are not deeply entrenched within us, it will be difficult for us to fake a creative, loving response. Military commanders or police captains would never push a recruit into a conflict situation without months and perhaps years of training. The same is true of waging peace. It takes study of Scripture, prayer, and, if possible, a support group to show us alternative options to violence.

A counterculture idea

In our culture creative, nonviolent responses to conflict are suspect. Rambo toys are the models for our children. Some Vietnam vets blame the "peaceniks" for prolonging the war. Conscientious objectors are seen by some as unpatriotic. Very few in our country would echo a statement from the Fellowship of Reconciliation: "Because of my faith I will agree to live in a nation without nuclear weapons." Our government identifies "enemies" or nations we are to mistrust. Blessing enemies and praying for those who try to harm us is a counterculture idea. Yet Jesus said, "Love your enemies, do good to those who hate you, bless those who curse you, pray for those who mistreat you" (Luke 6:27-28). This seems like naive idealism. We judge that our enemies are not lovable people. They make us angry and afraid. We assume they want to harm us. So why love them? Yet our parent-God says to us, "Love your enemies because I told you to. I loved you when you were my enemies. Can I not expect as much from you?"

Is that answer enough for us? Most of us rebelled at strong parental commands, only to discover later in life that our parents had our best interests at heart. Our participation in the kingdom of God depends on our ability to love not just our friends, but to love our enemies. We do not earn our way into that realm of God by loving, but love is the essence of God's kingdom. God is love. God's rule is indiscriminate love.

This is frightening for us, because to love the enemy rather than retaliate makes us vulnerable. We feel stripped and naked, relying only on the promise that nothing can separate us from God's love, or the promise that in life and in death we belong to God. Promises such as "Surely I am with you always, to the very end of the age" (Matt. 28:20) seem naive when we are facing an assailant. "My grace is sufficient for you, for my power is made perfect in weakness" (2 Cor. 12:9) is a word from Jesus I may have in my mind, but I do not know it by *heart*.

When we begin to trust these promises and know them *by heart*, we are free to be creative in our responses to violence and conflict. The energy we use in hating and devising ways of getting even can be directed toward the radical idea of blessing our enemies, as Jesus asks us to do. To bless them is to want the very best for them. Our goal is to elicit from them the person God created them to be. To evoke their goodness and be reconciled to them is the vision of *shalom* God has for us. It is the vision of unity and wholeness. It is peace.

There is an ongoing theological debate about whether human beings are basically good or evil. The following story does not end the debate but it sheds some light on the practice of nonviolence.

A holy man sat near a river in India. He had come to meditate near an ancient tree that had spread out its roots to meet the water. The roots had been exposed when the water eroded the soil around them. On one root the old man noticed a scorpion clinging to the wood for its very life. Time and again the water would lap over the root and threaten to drown the creature.

The old man knelt beside the roots and reached out to rescue the scorpion. Each time he would grab for the scorpion it tried to sting him.

A young man came by and observed what the old man was trying to do. "Foolish old man," said the younger man. "Don't you realize the scorpion will continue to sting you?"

The old man replied, "Just because it is the nature of the scorpion to sting does not mean that I have to change my nature, which is to save."

Saving is a central message of Christianity. Jesus widened our definition of salvation and our concept of those who were to be loved. Not an eye for an eye, or even love of neighbor, was what our Savior asked, but, "Love your enemies."

All animals have a survival instinct and a desire to protect family. By the grace of God we humans were given the ability to think creatively, to learn new ways of protection. We are asked to include even our enemies in those savings acts. God did.

8

By living conscientiously and simply so that I do not deprive others of the means to live . . .

A WONDERFUL WORD— ENOUGH

All things by immortal power
hiddenly
together linked are
thou cannot disturb a flower
without troubling a star.
                    Francis Thompson

One Christmas we treated ourselves to a stage performance of *A Christmas Carol* by Charles Dickens. As we watched the Bob Cratchit family enjoying their Christmas dinner, complete with a goose supplied by an anonymous donor, the narrator observed, "For once the Cratchit family had enough. What a wonderful word—enough!"

Enough. Others have also understood the beauty and the freedom of that word.

"Give me neither poverty nor riches; feed me with the food that is needful for me" (Prov. 30:8 RSV).

"Give us today our daily bread," Jesus prayed (Matt. 6:11).

God's word to the Israelites in the wilderness was that they should only gather as much manna as they needed (Exodus 16).

"I have learned to be content whatever the circumstances," wrote Paul (Phil. 4:11).

"Anything you take more than you need, you have stolen from someone else," said St. Augustine.

Where do these radical ideas originate? They are not the tenets of an economic system in which manufactured needs are met with manufactured goods. They are not slogans dreamed up by ad consultants who show a "cosmopolitan girl" in a full page ad sharing her feelings that "moderation is just about the dullest philosophy I ever heard."

They contradict the dominant view among leaders of American industry that we have a basic human right to live in luxury and enjoy what we have "earned." Over and over again we are told "Go ahead. You deserve it."

This view assaults us every day through the advertising media of print and television. Advertisers assure us that we should go ahead and enjoy the fruits of our "good old Yankee ingenuity" without being overly concerned about what happens to anyone else.

What we are asked to believe is that salvation comes through the consumption of goods and services, that the "good life" exists only for those who have much more than they need and can afford to flaunt it in the face of those who have little or nothing.

Advertisers themselves often recognize how blatantly theological their message is. Sometimes they even try to capitalize on the connection by using religious vocabulary or by making references to Christian themes. For example, self-denial may be mentioned, but only as irrational behavior to be avoided at all costs. And the word *sin* has become synonymous with pleasure. Products that are to be desired are routinely presented as "positively sinful" or "sinfully delicious."

Shalom as subversive

The philosophy of "enough" certainly contradicts our assumption that enough is never enough. If the polls are right, our self-worth as North Americans is intricately linked with the number of things we own.

The philosophy of enough is not a philosophy but a faith issue for Christians. Throughout Scripture we are presented with the radical idea of sufficiency as a God-pleasing way to live. God has a vision and a plan to sustain all that was and is created. The vision is *shalom.*

Shalom is the beautiful Hebrew word we translate as "peace." Peace means different things to different people. The English word for peace comes from the Latin word *Pax.* Pax has mainly to do with the absence of war, an agreement not to fight. To a person from India, peace is *shanti* and implies a state of inner contentment. We have already seen that *ping,* the Chinese word for peace, includes the necessity of balance, things held in equilibrium. In Russian, the word for peace is *mir* and is also the word for world. Peace evidently includes the environment and global well-being.

It is more difficult to define *shalom.*

It means material well-being and prosperity. "I was envious when I saw the *shalom* of the wicked," the psalmist wrote.

Shalom stones—smooth, round, and unchipped—were to be gathered to build an altar.

Shalom means physical and mental health. "Is your father *shalom*?" Joseph asked his brothers when he saw them in Egypt.

If you and I were Jews and met on the street and I said, "Is it *shalom* with you today?" I would be asking if you had food and clothing, a job, and money to pay your bills. You could answer, "Yes, it is *shalom* with me today," or, like many in our global family, you might say, "No, it isn't *shalom* with me today. I am poor and hungry, in ill health and without a job. My life is not filled with peace. It is not *shalom.*"

Shalom is a many-faceted word, but this word for peace, like peace itself, embraces a wholeness and sense of unity and justice. God's plan of *shalom* includes the economics, the political aspirations, the sexuality, the food and drink, the vocations, and the prayer life of God's people.

In all of the more than 200 times *shalom* is used in the Old Testament, it is never an individual or private concept. *Shalom* is always used in a communal context, in the context of a people. It is not a private peace between one individual and God. *Shalom* is social. I cannot be at peace if you are not at peace. There cannot be peace unless righteousness and justice prevail. Can we begin to envision a world in which everyone has enough and none have more than they need?

Doing justice

Injustice is the basis of most of the anger and frustration in the world. Much of the injustice is the result of racism, of greed, of economic systems that cater to the rich. These things are not new to the human race. James wrote in his epistle:

What causes wars, and what causes fightings among you? Is it not your passions that are at war in your members? You desire and do not have; so you kill. And you covet and cannot obtain; so you fight and wage war. You do not have, because you do not ask. You ask and do not receive, because you ask wrongly, to spend it on your passions. (James 4:1-3 RSV).

I don't like to hear that my consumer instincts allow me to "satisfy my passions." I prefer to describe the way I live in such phrases as "mastering the possibilities," "my world should know no limits," "taking advantage of cultural opportunities," "enhancing my education," "enjoying the variety of goods and services available to me," "keeping up with what is fashionable so as not to look dumpy," "freeing up my time with machines that are more convenient," or "a reward for hard work and productivity."

To justify my consumerism, advertisements even appeal to my responsibility as a parent. If I choose a solidly built, expensive, well-made car, it is not for my sake but for the sake of my children. Certain tires will protect a child more than others. "Your kids deserve the best," I'm told.

I write this as a white, middle-class citizen of a first-world nation. It is difficult to stand back and objectively critique a system from which I benefit and in which I am enmeshed. As Christians, we need to critique it, however, and see the connections between the way we live and our global family.

What we consider the good life in the United States directly affects people in other nations. The coffee, the sugar, the fruits and vegetables we consume in the winter, the plastics and other petroleum products, the copper and other metals used in the manufacture of gadgets to make our life easier—these products often come from third and fourth-world countries where labor is cheap, where people are exploited, where people are hungry because land is used for export products. It is not a simple problem. World economics and trade are complicated issues. It is not a complicated issue, however, to see how closely linked our life-styles are to others. Those of us who believe in a God who created the world and pronounced it good, a God who made enough for all, can understand the meaning of that wonderful word—*enough*.

The prophet Micah wrote, "What does the Lord require of you but to do justice and to love kindness and to walk humbly with your God?" (Micah 6:8 RSV). How do we "do justice" in our lives?

Depending on your gifts and interests, you may choose to work for justice through advocacy and political action—working to change unjust laws or policies that foster hunger and oppression in the world. Perhaps you choose nonviolent resistance, joining a protest action at a weapons plant or refusing to pay the portion of your taxes that goes to build arms. You may boycott certain products to protest unfair labor practices or to symbolize solidarity with people in underdeveloped nations. You may volunteer to work in a shelter, in a home for abused mothers and children. You may take in foster children. Perhaps you can help hurting people most directly through your vocation.

Whatever way you choose, there is one way to do justice in which we can all participate. Begin where you have the most power to act—in your life-style.

In the vow of nonviolence we promised to live simply so as not to deprive others of the means to live. This is a middle-class luxury. We can choose at any time to live differently, while many of the world's people live simply, because they have no choice.

Most of us are well-educated and can find a fulfilling job. We are willing to live with inconveniences, but at any point we can draw the line and say, "So much for inconvenience! I'm buying a car or a different coat. I'll travel when and where I like, eat from the great variety of food at the co-op or supermarket, and attend the college of my choice. I'll give the children music lessons, sports opportunities, and cultural advantages, no matter what the cost. If the winter months get long, there is nothing to stop me from buying a VCR to ease the boredom."

We *try* to live simply. It is an everyday struggle, and we need constant nurture and renewal of our commitment. We try to make global connections, because we are convinced it is anti-*shalom* to live with our consumer values in a world of severe maldistribution of wealth. Trying to live simply is one way to "do justice."

It's hard to change

Old habits are hard to break. In small steps we have increased what we think of as needs. We have made our happiness dependent on "stuff."

In *Redbook* magazine a mother told how she and her young child had gone to the store to buy disposable diapers. She was complaining to her four-year-old about always having to get in the car and drive to the store to buy the diapers for the new baby. The child looked up at her and with a big smile said, "Wouldn't it be wonderful if someone invented a diaper that you could wash out and use over again?"

Any talk of simplicity of life-style raises the ire and defenses of many of us. It hits us where few other justice activities do. It asks *us* to change.

When we write to our congressperson about a justice concern, we expect the government to change. We blame the president and want him to do something different to promote justice. If we refuse to pay a portion of our income tax because it goes to manufacture weapons, the government may take the money from our bank account, but the inconvenience seems small. Even in protest actions, we are asking someone else to change.

For me, trying to live more simply has proven to be the greater challenge for justice work. It cannot be a substitute for other justice agendas or separated from advocacy for the poor, but it lays the foundation for our connectedness to others. It is a small step that helps us identify with so many who have so little. It is a symbol to help us carry their needs in our hearts.

Living simply involves many daily decisions. Will this purchase really satisfy a *need* that I have? Am I freely making this choice, or has someone else convinced me I need it? British ad artist Kenneth Bromfield wrote, "From any cross section of ads, the general advertiser's attitude would seem to be: if you are lousy, smelly, idle, underprivileged, an oversexed-status-seeking neurotic moron, give me your money." And we do!

Let's face it. We're addicts. Let's admit we have a problem and get help. Ernest Becker observed: "We drink or drug ourselves into oblivion or we go shopping which is the same thing" (*Denial of Death*, Free Press, 1973).

Begin by making a *shalom* life-style list of needs. Be specific. What is *enough* in the way of clothing, travel, housing, leisure expenditures? No one's list will be the same. My needs may not be the same as your needs, but our lists will be more honest if we remember that God created a world with enough for everyone. New economic orders can begin with a grass-roots faith question: What is enough?

Nobel Peace Prize winner, Jane Addams said, "The good we secure for ourselves is precarious and uncertain . . . until it is secured for all of us and incorporated into our common life."

Change is difficult, but just imagine a world where everyone had enough!

The freedom of sufficiency

Life-style changes are more appealing if we begin with those that give us freedom. In what areas of life do we feel the things we have control us? It is not freeing to be a slave to the things we own—trying to maintain that boat we rarely use, worrying about that second vacation house standing empty much of the year, worrying over investments, polishing, cleaning, preserving things we seldom use.

Maybe we overestimated the size of the house we needed, and the mortgage payments are a burden. We rationalize that we need a place to accommodate the collection of things the children may someday want. But one day we die, and our children are left with boxes and crates and trunks full of things they don't need and never would have missed. You can begin now to deaccumulate.

The argument that more gadgets and newer toys will free us to spend more time for the important things of life is just not true. My experience has been that the day we got a dishwasher we stopped having some good family time over the dishpan. The time I save I waste. Television addiction has stifled our creativity and cut off good conversation. Gadgets break, and most of them seem to be encased in plastic and have to be thrown away. Our lust to have more and newer time-saving devices is a disease of a consumer culture. Dis-ease: feeling strangely uncomfortable that all the resources needed to produce and maintain the things for which I lust somehow take away from someone else's needs.

We share a world where there is enough. When I ask my sisters and brothers, "Is it *shalom* with you today," I want them to be able to say, "Yes, it is." If they say no, I want to be able to share with them what has been entrusted to me.

If the need for two salaries is causing family stress and making a new vocation or a move impossible, consider reassessing your needs. Life-style changes are meant to enable us to live with compassion for others and to feel a sense of freedom, not deprivation.

Jesus came to proclaim release to the captives. It is easy to be seduced into captivity, but more difficult to realize that we are captives. Freedom for us, as well as for our brothers and sisters, can be learning to live with an understanding of sufficiency.

Life as gift

Life is good as it is given. God's good gifts are meant to fill us with a sense of joy. Living simply can heighten this joy, because our sense of well-being will not be determined by our successes or an accumulation of consumer items.

When our daughter was young, I watched her struggle to put together her first puzzle. The toy drawer was full of pieces from an assortment of different puzzles, and her first task was to separate out the ones that fit together to complete the landscape picture. I could tell she was frustrated by pieces that were missing and even more frustrated when she tried to push larger pieces into place that didn't belong there. I also remember the joy in her voice when she looked up and said, "Look, mommy. It all fits together. Everything is right."

Perhaps the apostle Paul was thinking of a puzzle when he used the Greek word *epieikes* in Philippians 4:5, "Let your *epieikes* be evident to all." *Epieikes* can be translated "fitting in." Let your "fitting in" be seen by all people. God's world is a puzzle where each of us is a small but important piece in the design. In the providence of God it all fits together.

The joy of abundant life comes when we see life as gift. The writer of Proverbs knew that too much and too little was dangerous for our spiritual and physical health.

> Give me neither poverty nor riches; feed me with the food that is needful for me, lest I be full, and deny thee, and say, "Who is the Lord?" or lest I be poor, and steal, and profane the name of my God.
>
> (Prov. 30:8-9 RSV)

Too much, too fast, too often make us callused and insensitive to God's good gifts and robs us of a sense of celebration. The things in life that at one time brought us joy and excitement we now regard as expected. Boredom sets in, and what once energized us now is met with a yawn and a casual, "So what?"

I remember the first time my parents were going to take me out for a restaurant meal. The anticipation itself was wonderful! When the evening finally came, the thought of that exciting event caused such bad stomach cramps that we had to postpone going out. I almost regret that now the thought of a restaurant meal no longer sends my stomach into spasms, and I go out to eat with a sense of indifference.

There is a prayer by Joseph Pintauro that hangs in our kitchen. It is called the farm worker's prayer and helps to clarify for me the gifts of life.

> All we ask, O Lord, is to be safe from the rain,
> Just warm enough in winter to watch the snow with a smile,

Enough to eat so that our hunger will not turn us into
    hungry beasts,
And sanity enough to make a justice that will not kill our
    love of life.

What a wonderful word—*enough.* Try it on for size.
It will fit you well.

9

By actively resisting the evils of oppressive structures and the causes of war . . .

OUR GOD IS A GOD OF JUSTICE

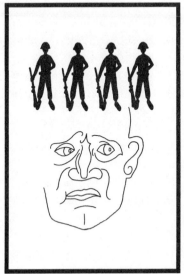

*Peace is not the absence of tension but
the presence of justice.*
Martin Luther King Jr.

One day an elderly woman walked slowly into St. Martin's Table, the bookstore/restaurant where I work. I was on my knees rearranging books in the peace/war section. She watched me for a few minutes and then came over and said, "What is the single most important thing I can do to stop war?"

I sat back on my heels and grinned at her. "Are you serious?" I asked, giving one of those laughs we reserve for people who ask ridiculous questions.

"Your literature says you're a peace-education center. I just want to know what I should be doing." She was very serious.

I looked over at my coworker for help but Judy was smiling and had her head tipped and eyebrows up, as if to say, "O.K., Smarty, what's your answer?"

A variety of answers raced through my head. Be a Joshua and walk around the Pentagon blowing trumpets for seven days until the walls fall down. Throw yourself in front of the white train that carries nuclear weapons back and forth across the United States. Do what young Samantha Smith did: journey to the Soviet Union to make friends with the Russian people. Refuse to pay the large percentage of your federal tax dollar that goes to build weapons. Climb the fence at a plant that manufactures weapons. Camp outside your congressional delegate's door until your concerns are heard. Pray, write letters, march, make noises, pray some more.

I felt humble and inarticulate. What does one say to an 80-year-old woman who seriously wants to stop war? I think I mumbled something about addressing the one issue about which she felt most deeply. God had given her gifts and talents that could be used to work for justice in any number of areas. I knew my stammerings were not sufficient, and I went back to rearranging my peace/war books realizing my inadequacies as a peace educator. None of my answers would have satisfied the woman's sincere question to me.

The question stayed with me. It wasn't until later that day that I began to think of the vow of nonviolence I had taken: "Before God the Creator and the sanctifying Spirit, I vow to carry out in my life the love and example of Jesus . . . by actively resisting the evils of oppressive structures and the causes of war." Perhaps this part of the vow would be a place for all of us to start a discussion. Together we could confess our complicity in the oppressive systems and structures that cause war. Maybe we could eventually see a way to begin to disengage our lives from those powers that control us.

Systems that shatter *shalom*

The dictionary defines a system as a "coordinated body of methods, or a complex scheme or plan of procedure." It seems that the more complex a system becomes, the more it tends to divide people, instead of unite them. Economic, political, or religious systems in themselves are not evil, but when a system causes divisions among the people of God, it is a fallen structure in need of redemption. God's *shalom* vision of unity and wholeness cannot coexist with unjust structures that make us fearful and suspicious of one another.

After Methodist theologian Jose Migues Bonino from Argentina addressed an overflow crowd at a local college, an earnest, middle-aged man stood up at the floor microphone and said: "We have a house and a car and a fairly good life. I can see how multinational corporations and certain governments are oppressors, but what about us? How does your theology view us middle-class, white Americans?"

Miguez Bonino was very gentle in his answer. "You are beneficiaries of an oppressive system. It's hard for you to break away from that system. I don't want you to respond with guilt. That would be remorse unto death rather than repentance unto life. What we do call for is that you be responsible. I hope that responsibility is exercised with joy."

"Beneficiaries of an oppressive system." I didn't choose to be born into a beneficiary role, but when I took the name of Christ as the one who controls my life, I became responsible for my global family. I became responsible for those who do not reap the benefits of systems under which I live. Our task is not so much to give of our surplus as it is to let go of what rightfully belongs to others. The rights and dignity of others include freedom from fear, adequate food and shelter, health care, jobs, and the right to choose their own form of government.

Oppressive systems that cause war are many, but let's briefly look at three: racism, unjust economic systems, and militarism.

Racism and unjust economic systems

In the United States we have a long history of plundering and of protecting and advancing our interests as first-world citizens. The Pilgrims believed they had a mandate from God to enter this promised land and make democracy a light on a hill and an example for other nations. It did not matter if others already lived on the land. Indians and Mexicans dare not impede progress. When white people reached the Pacific Ocean and there was no more land to possess, we transferred our manifest destiny to people and land beyond our shores.

One of the greatest holocausts in human history occurred when slave traders brought African blacks to this country. A low estimate is that 40 million people died as a result of transporting slaves to America. Sharks followed the ships across the ocean, feeding on human flesh. The price in human life is staggering when we realize we are beneficiaries of a system of exploitation and human pain.

After the civil-rights legislation in the late 1960s many of us felt at least one problem was solved, one wrong system made right. And yet racism continues to exploit and oppress. Employment figures do not reflect the story of young black males, who suffer 40% unemployment. Statistics do not show that in New York state, 56% of the Native Americans living there are without jobs. The health status of American Indians lags 20-25 years behind white society, and infant mortality on Indian reservations and in our nation's capital equals that of many third and fourth-world countries.

News stories do not always reveal the racist attitudes of employers, law-enforcement systems, churches, fellow workers, and teachers. Our stereotypes betray our prejudices and keep us from looking into the root causes of injustice. Not everyone in our own country benefits from the system that serves some of us so well.

One example brings the reality of this to my consciousness. My friend Jaimie is a nurse at a county hospital. One day a 19-year-old Native American woman was brought into the emergency room. She had been found in an alley off Franklin Avenue unconscious, the result of an overdose of drugs. The young woman was pregnant and went into labor, delivering a tiny infant who was addicted to the drug. In the previous year the woman had given birth to another child who was brain damaged at birth because of the mother's addiction.

I thought of my own daughter, who is pregnant with her first child. From the day she found out she was going to have a baby, Karen has not had caffeine, alcohol, or even an aspirin. I tease her about her fussiness, but she just smiles and tells me she wants their baby to have the best start possible in life.

I cry out at the injustice, at a system that allows some mothers to be caught in a life of poverty, low self-esteem, and drugs to erase the misery of their lives. How does this happen? I want to place the blame somewhere—on the young woman's parents, grandparents, the government, the city, God. Or do we, somehow, share in the responsibility?

To resist an oppressive system, we need to be aware of injustice. Unless we put ourselves in positions where we come in contact with the poor, with those who are hurting, with the victims, we will feel no responsibility and will not have the compassion necessary to pick up one small piece of the problem and work for change.

The victims of our systems are the most vulnerable of God's family and therefore need our compassion. As soon as I find myself separating God's family into "we" and "they," I know this is a signal to take a hard look at the structures and institutions under which we live.

My son-in-law, Jim, who grew up in South Africa, went back there to visit. Jim saw little change in the dehumanization caused by the apartheid system. Not long afterward we watched a news report on television about the one million South Africans who are without homes after shanty towns and refugee settlements were razed by the government. We saw the violence not only to the bodies but to the spirits of the parents who looked at us from the television screen. Mothers had no milk for crying babies; fathers could not provide food and medical help for their families. The despair of these sisters and brothers is the result of a system of separation that has for years been supported by worldwide economic interests.

The television report broke for an ad for cat food. I was reminded again that our pets live better than many children in the world today. Our cats are fed nutritious, well-balanced meals from a can, given milk and a warm place to sleep, and taken to the vet when they are ill.

The documentary continued. An old truck rolled into the area where the blacks were being resettled. On the back of the truck were a dozen people trying to keep a large drainage pipe from rolling off. This was to be home for the family. Later the cameras showed a canvas stretched over one end of the pipe to add to the sleeping space. There was one well in the settlement, where, in ankle deep mud, the children waited in line to fill containers with water.

I was embarrassed for the advertisers who had purchased the two minutes following this segment. Viewers were shown the newest appliances that helped to "make our life a little easier." Microwaves, dishwashers, and clothes dryers flashed on the screen. I wondered what would help to make the life of my South African family "a little easier."

Next followed an ad for windows—the bubble-bath window above the opulent tub, the Sunday morning family-time windows that enclosed the porch, the double windows that keep cold out in the winter and heat out in the summer. I found myself weeping at the injustice and the disparity so glaringly contrasted. I remembered the words of poet James Carroll: "When anything dies a little, we all die a lot."

William Faulkner's words also drummed in my head: "Some things you must always be unable to bear . . . injustice and outrage and dishonor and shame. No matter how young you are or how old . . . just refuse to bear them."

How do we refuse to bear the injustice? When does concern become compassion? It happens when we begin to make connections, when we begin to realize that we are family—God's family. When part of my family is hurting and dying because of systems of greed and superiority, prejudice and fear, repentance is called for. Real change follows real conversion, which follows forgiveness, which is a result of repentance.

When I once helped plan an interfaith worship service, one man was upset about the litany of confession we had proposed. "It is morbid and psychologically harmful," he said. My experience has always been just the opposite. It isn't that our confession brings God's grace, but that God's grace frees us to be honest and repentant. However, for most of us, confession has to do mostly with private sins and rarely with our corporate sin. The confession of corporate guilt is also the result of accepting the grace of God. It is the beginning of "repentance unto life."

Economics and the gospel

"What causes wars among you?" the letter of James asks. Is it not our greed? There has not been much talk in the religious communities of our country about the competition and self-advancement that undergirds our socioeconomic system. The pastoral letter on the economy by the Roman Catholic bishops, *Economic Justice for All*, is the rare exception.

The bishops ask us to take a look at our unrestrained competition for material advantage. They challenge our love affair with the profit motive, and show this ethic as being contrary to the gospel. The bishops point out that the first public words of Jesus informed his listeners that he was appointed by God "to preach good news to the poor" and to "proclaim freedom for the prisoners" (Luke 4:18). The bishops wrote a letter of concern by describing the world not from a corporate office but from a soup kitchen, because they are committed to the gospel of Christ. "They are taking Jesus seriously, and we are not accustomed to doing this," commented Michael Harrington. He wrote: "Some people feel the Bishops are creeping socialists hiding behind their pectoral crosses. . . . It is profoundly wrong to describe their letter as socialist. For the astonishing and simple fact is that this document is, above all, religious. They are not socialist, just Christian," concluded Harrington (commentary page, Minneapolis Star and Tribune, Nov. 24, 1986).

The gospel of Jesus should remind us that the good life as defined by many in our country cannot also be the good life for the rest of humanity. As heavy as this all seems to us, we cannot deny that as beneficiaries of an unjust system of economics, our life-style dehumanizes others. Suffering brought on another because of injustice is a cross imposed on some of God's people. Latin American theologian Leonard Boff writes:

> Since God was crucified in Jesus Christ, no cross imposed unjustly is a matter of indifference to him. Jesus is in solidarity with all those who hang on crosses. Their humiliation is his humiliation. They do not carry their crosses by themselves. Jesus carries it with them and in them.

It is in the victim, in the poor and oppressed, that we align ourselves with the compassionate God. "Jesus is God made poor," wrote Jim Wallis. Jesus made it very clear that when he comes again, our spiritual temperature will not be judged by how pious or religious we have been. Jesus will ask: Did you give drink to those who were thirsty and food to the hungry? Did you visit the prisoners, practice hospitality, and clothe those who had little or nothing to wear? If so, says Jesus, you ministered to me (Matthew 25).

When James gives an alternative to greed, it is a prayer of trust. "You do not have because you do not ask." Faith is letting go of our will as well as our fears, and laying at God's feet our complete trust—the times when we lack the things we need and the times of abundance, acknowledging that all we are and have is gift.

Militarism

Militarism is defined as "the tendency to regard military efficiency as the supreme ideal of the state, and to subordinate all other interests to those of the military."

A December 1986 Gallop poll announced: "Public losing confidence in the church." For the first time in more than a decade the church had lost its primary place as the institution in which Americans have the greatest confidence. First place now goes to the military. That is where we put our trust.

It is inevitable that the more we have, the more we have to protect. Many of the more wealthy suburbs now have gateways leading in and a guard posted to screen visitors. The more we possess, the higher our fences become. A safe is installed, a gun is kept in the bedroom, the watch dog is larger, and ulcers are more pronounced.

On the international front, we compete for weapon superiority because our global interests are vulnerable. We protect our American way of life with arms that can kill rather than arms that reach out to offer economic justice and compassion.

We would find much less need of protection, if we could define abundant life in terms of gifts rather than possessions: gifts like the music of Mozart, ice cream cones, candlelight, bike paths, people to love, tomatoes from the garden, little children, granola, the smell of newly mown hay, beaches at sunset, a fulfilling job, Christmas trees, baseball. All of these good things are a small part of the life system that took billions of years to develop, and we are the first generation of people who have the capacity to totally destroy everything on earth.

Even though more and more of us are finding that U.S. defense expenditures are unacceptable, we feel caught in a system of militarism that seems to be beyond our responsibility. Yet with 40-60% of our federal tax dollar going to pay for the debt on past wars and present military spending, we cannot absolve ourselves of our complicity in the arms race. Each of us who fills out an income-tax form and sends in a check to the government helps to pay for the weapons.

These weapons then become our security. They are our trust-point and therefore become an idol. In *By Faith Alone* (Holden Village, 1983) Dan Erlander points out that we make inordinate sacrifices to this idol. The idol undermines our economic security, because military spending is inflationary. We make a product we hope we never use. Sophisticated weapon building creates fewer jobs than the same amount of money spent on health, education, construction, or human services.

We sacrifice human life in the developing nations, where most of our wars are now fought. We sacrifice our environment and the resources of the earth. We sacrifice the poor in ghettos and on reservations—mostly women and children. We sacrifice the lives of our sons and husbands, brothers and fathers, in war. When we choose to keep the peace through strength with a "lion mentality," we must be aware of the sacrifices we make. Not only is it costly, but there are no winners in modern warfare—only losers.

Peace through strength is not a new concept. God's people often trusted in their own strength rather than putting their trust solely in God. The prophets admonished the Israelites:

> You have planted wickedness, you have reaped evil, you have eaten the fruit of deception. Because you have depended on your own strength and on your many warriors, the roar of battle will arise against your people, so that all your fortresses will be devastated (Hos. 10:13-14).

Isaiah also had harsh pronouncements:

> Woe to those who go down to Egypt for help, who rely on horses, who trust in the multitude of their chariots

and in the great strength of their horsemen, but do not look to the Holy One of Israel, or seek help from the Lord! (Isa. 31:1).

Trust is a frightening concept. It changes the lion mentality to that of a lamb. It is following, not knowing where we are going, but believing only that God's ways and God's strength will be our security. Trust is not a passive stance. It is active nonviolence, taking Jesus at his word when he says to let go of our idea of security and follow him. Jesus is calling us by his life and his words into a different kind of security, into ways that promote reconciliation instead of hostility.

Surely the best way to prevent war is to heal the underlying causes of fear and hatred. Military power is an admission that we have failed to be compassionate, a confession that violence has influenced God's people more than God's people have influenced violence. Injustice is always the root cause of war.

To proclaim the gospel is to say that you can trust the Word. God is trustworthy.

Some small first steps

Stepping out of the system from which we North Americans benefit seems as easy as walking on water. Everywhere we turn we find ourselves trapped in the structures of our politics, economics, and culture. We begin to feel like the man who took a walk one day and met a lion, so he quickly turned down another path but met a bear. Thinking "This is not my day," he ran for home, leaned exhausted against the wall, and was bitten by a snake! (Amos 5:19).

We tend to be so overwhelmed that we do nothing. We can't see how one small step is going to make any difference. But God encourages each of our "small faiths" and can use every small effort we make. God must surely smile when one person becomes aware of the fractured vision of *shalom* and begins to resist, in some way, the sinful systems of injustice.

Since the Community of St. Martin took the vow of nonviolence, some concerns have been surfacing among the members.

Sue began to investigate where she had her savings invested—a reliable denominational fund. She discovered they were not as socially responsible as she had thought. This discovery prompted several of us to set up a meeting with an investment manager to learn about funds that provide alternative places to invest our savings. We have learned there are firms who will guide us away from investing in companies who manufacture weapon components or who excessively pollute the environment. It is not necessary to choose between a financial goal and ethical standards. At the end of this chapter are suggestions and information if you wish to pursue this way of actively resisting unjust systems.

There is a growing number of our community who are war-tax resisters. They see tax resistance as a way to be conscientious objectors to war even if they are not males between the ages of 18 and 25. Others keep their income below the taxable level and try to channel their monies into places of human need. There is no pure place to stand, but for some, refusing to pay all or a portion of their war tax is a way to say, "The arms build-up will stop with me." A bishop calls his tax resistance a "tea bag in the Boston Harbor." He has no delusions that this will bring about world peace, but what if all Christians began to do this?

Learn to know your neighbors. Learn to know the people who live on the margin of society in your community. What are the housing problems, the employment problems, the social problems that dehumanize those around you? When someone came to one of our community meetings and said, "What are we going to do about the battered women in our neighborhood?" I wanted to yell, "Don't tell me about one more injustice! I can't possibly take on one more problem." But each of us can pick up one part of one injustice and begin to make a difference, if only to one hurting person.

Believe in the power of prayer and begin to pray. In our worship we regularly pray for our enemies. It doesn't take long before they do not seem like enemies. When my prayers have lost touch with human need, I know I am not connected with my brothers and sisters. Our calling as people of God is to intercede for the helpless, the powerless, the victims of injustice. God teaches us how to pray by giving us the opportunity to share in the joy and pain of one another, so learn to know your neighbors.

We are called to respond not with remorse unto death, but with repentance unto life. Our God is a God of justice—costly justice, because we have much to lose, but even more to gain.

For further information:

Interfaith Center for Corporate Responsibility
475 Riverside Drive, Room 566
New York, NY 10115

This group coordinates church corporate responsibility work. It has a long list of alternatives in creative investments and social responsibility. It provides information on policies and practices of many companies.

Working Assets
230 California Street
San Francisco, CA 94111

A money-market fund founded in 1983 and dedicated exclusively to managing socially responsible investments, such as housing, renewable energy sources, family farms, and higher education.

Pax World Fund
224 State Street
Portsmouth, NH 03801

Established in 1970, this fund is a no-load, open-end, diversified mutual fund with both economic and social criteria. It endeavors to make a contribution to world peace through investing in companies producing life-supportive goods and services.

Directory of Socially Responsible Investments

A booklet containing socially screened securities, money-market funds, investment advisors and brokers. Also lists community investments and research and resource organizations. Order from Funding Exchange, 666 Broadway–5th Floor, New York, NY 10012.

Rating America's Corporate Conscience by Lyndenberg, Marlin, and Strub (Addison Wesley, 1987).

In conjunction with the Council on Economic Priorities, these authors have compiled an excellent, comprehensive guide on social responsibility. Over 125 major corporations are charted, showing charitable contributions, weapons contracts, women and minority representation in management, and environmental concerns.

Guide to War Tax Resistance by War Resister's League, 339 Layfayette St., New York, NY 10012.

A good manual on the politics and methods of war-tax resistance.

Add Justice to Your Shopping List by Marilyn Voran (Herald Press, 1986).

A booklet that examines our North American food production and distribution. A handy guide for reshaping our food buying habits.

World Military and Social Expenditures by Ruth Leger Sivard (World Priorities, Box 25140, Washington, DC 20007).

A factual report of the interconnectedness between rich and poor countries. Shows "overkill," instability, military excess, and social deficits.

10

By embracing the redemptive suffering of Jesus on the cross, accepting my own suffering which may result from active, nonviolent love, and being willing to enter into the suffering of others . . .

THE WORD OF THE CROSS IS THE POWER OF GOD

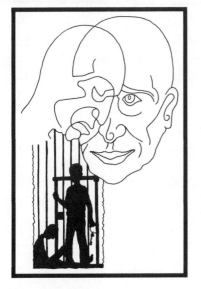

*God has promised to make better lovers
of us.*   James B. Nelson

I f it is difficult to love our enemies and drastically change our life-style, a vow to embrace suffering seems even more out of reach. One begins to feel that modeling Christ-like love is not possible for anyone except a few saints. Would any of us choose to suffer?

The original Pax Christi vow our community studied said: "I will accept suffering rather than inflict it." As the Women and Nonviolence group began to look closely at the idea of suffering, many took serious exception to the wording of the vow. The pain of abuse—both physical and emotional—was still vivid in the minds of some. Several of us knew of other women who had been beaten or otherwise abused by their parents or spouse. Often these women had sought counseling from a pastor and had been told it was their Christian duty to accept that suffering. As Christ accepted suffering, so must they. They were supposed to go back and try to make their husbands love them. And so these women had gone back to their Jekyll and Hyde spouses, trying to find that bit of magic to keep love alive.

Women shared stories of feeling battered by constant belittling of their ideas and by frequent destructive criticism that lowered their self-esteem. Some suffered the pain of dead relationships and told how their spouses had withdrawn from them emotionally.

We continued to ask the question of what is a non-violent response for a woman? If a woman is struck and does not respond, it is assumed that she is either too weak physically to strike back or that she is accepting a passive woman's role. However, if a man is struck in the face and refuses to retaliate, he may be commended for his nonviolent response. We were confronted again with the hard question of how to make nonviolent resistance the active, reconciling power it is.

What we women saw in this part of the Pax Christi vow was another example of passivity, that cultural trap women often accept. Too often we have confused *passivity* with the nonviolent, loving, active stance of *pacifism*. Because these two words are often confused, the women envisioned the possibility of this vow being used to tell women to be passive, to be victims.

As this discussion continued in the Community of St. Martin, we realized that the Christian faith has often been seen as masochistic. Extreme examples of severe austerity, hair shirts, self-inflicted beatings, or Martin Luther's lying naked in the snow came to mind as we remembered ways people tried to repent of sin or to find a gracious God. We rejected the idea, often unspoken, that if you're not suffering, God probably doesn't love you very much.

We also reminded ourselves that many times we deliberately choose life-styles that cause suffering. Emotional stress and physical illness come from overeating or undereating, overwork, drugs, alcohol, promiscuity, poor choice of friends, or other self-inflicted pain. We knew that the Pax Christi vow did not ask us to accept suffering as a way of atonement or self-inflicted suffering.

There were other problems, too. The original wording of the vow gave us two choices—to accept or to inflict suffering. Was there no other alternative? Someone suggested that if we were to follow Christ, the Christian was to "absorb hostility." The cruelty of the adversary can be brought to light by absorbing his or her blows without retaliation, but somehow this sponge image still didn't convey the power we felt important in nonviolent love.

Were we called to deflect violence and suffering? We imagined Wonder Woman in scanty garb and knee-high boots, brandishing a shiny shield to ward off arrows of pain and prevent any possible suffering. Wonder Woman never got hurt, nor did she change her heart or the heart of the aggressor. Maybe we were called to be martyrs, to lay down our shield and deliberately risk death whether or not God called us to such a sacrifice. Why was the suggestion of suffering in the vow? we wondered.

Take up your cross

Our discussions were long and intense, and we wondered if we were unwilling to admit the radical nature of the way of the cross. A cross is something we wear around our neck or reflect on during worship. No one wants to hang on one. Yet Jesus asked us to take up our cross and follow him. At the heart of our faith is the cross, so it is important to understand what it means.

The cross was the enfleshment of absolute, nonviolent, self-giving love. Jesus suffered by choice, not as some masochistic act, but as a way to disarm the powers of evil. He chose to incarnate what he had spent a lifetime teaching: love of enemies, absolute trust in God, and faith that his suffering would be transformed into power. The cross was the most visible sign of how God chose to relate to enemies—not by destroying them but by meeting them with extravagant love, even to the point of suffering and death.

For Jesus the cross was the result of a life that ran headlong into the values of the world, and the collision shook eternity. The cross sealed the reconciliation of each of us to God and each of us to one another, even our enemies.

How does this theology translate into our lives? Let's go back to the discussion of women who seem to respond passively to violent situations. We have already seen that passivity and nonviolence are very different responses. When one is suffering, it is important to understand the difference. Have I chosen to suffer? Am I suffering by choice, because of a faith stance I have taken? Suffering that is laid on us through injustice, by a drunk or violent spouse, or through the denial of our human rights is never the will of God. To accept this kind of suffering is to participate in the violence. However, if we decide to love and therefore to respond with nonviolence, we may suffer consequences. We may be taken advantage of, called naive or unrealistic, or ridiculed. We may experience more violence. This is suffering which results from a deliberate choice to meet hatred with love, indifference with concern, and violence with nonviolent responses. The active love and concern is what makes a response nonviolent rather than passive.

An abused woman realized that allowing her husband to continue to harm her was participating in his violence. One day after being violently abused she called the police and pressed charges. Her husband was convicted and sentenced to jail. Every day the wife went to visit her husband, saying, "I love you, but not your violence. I promise I will visit you every day while you serve your sentence, and I will wait for your release. I will not leave you, and because I love you, I won't let you be violent to me anymore."

This kind of loving does not mean that we remain victims. It is the result of our claiming God's Spirit deep in our center. From that center we can love with a God-like love and forgive with a Christ-like forgiveness. When we embrace the redemptive suffering of Jesus on the cross, we acknowledge that there is real, redemptive power in suffering. Hearts can be changed, because non-violent suffering can be a very powerful social force. When we respond with violence, we inflict suffering on another. If we make a choice to accept suffering by refusing to hate, the lesson is clear to even the simplest person.

The role of suffering continues to be an ongoing discussion in the Community of St. Martin. We rewrote this part of the vow so that it more clearly focused the intent of suffering: "I vow to carry out in my life the love and example of Jesus . . . by embracing the redemptive suffering of Jesus on the cross, accepting my own suffering which may result from active, nonviolent love, and being willing to enter into the suffering of others."

Examples of this kind of suffering are not difficult to find. Mary Nelson, who directs a housing ministry in Chicago, tells of walking in a civil-rights demonstration with singer Mahalia Jackson. A woman standing along the curb came up to Mahalia with eyes full of hate, seething with anger, and spit a huge glob of saliva in Mahalia's face. The singer wiped her face with her hand, smiled at the woman, and said, "God bless you, my child." Mary said, "That's when I first knew what power was all about!"

Mahalia's actions were not passive. They came from a deep center of self-worth and acceptance of her call to be a follower of Jesus Christ. Because of this call she had chosen to be part of a nonviolent demonstration that unmasked racial violence and prejudice. She did not retaliate, but accepted the humiliation with grace and a word of blessing.

Not everyone responds with such grace. In 1968 my husband John took nonviolence training before he participated in the Poor People's March in Washington, D.C. Among the participants of the training was a very large black pastor who had been a professional boxer. During the course of the day John lost track of the man, but as he was leaving later in the afternoon, he saw the pastor.

"How's it going?" John asked.

"Not good at all," came the reply. "I flunked. The first time one of the trainers called me 'boy,' I felt my hand become a fist and my jaw stiffen. I'd never have made it if this had been the real thing."

I liked the pastor's honesty. Most of us may think we are nonviolent people, but we never put ourselves into situations where we discover if we are or not. We open ourselves up to the possibility of God's Spirit working in us through prayer, practice, discipline, and extravagant love.

Suffering that empowers

There is great power in redemptive suffering. Within this kind of suffering is the possibility of disarming the heart and mind of the assailant. God can use redemptive suffering for the conversion of both the victim and the aggressor.

Manuel was from Central America and lived in New York City. He was a quiet person, who ran a small business in the Bronx. He was always helpful to his customers and neighbors.

After he had been in the United States for some time and had learned to trust a few friends, he told them why he had come to New York. He had been with the secret police in his country, and his job had been to torture political prisoners. He did not enjoy what he was ordered to do, but his training had been thorough, and he thought very little of going into a cell to interrogate and torture his victim. It was a job, like any other job.

One prisoner, however, disturbed him greatly. Every time he entered the prisoner's cell, the man would look at him and smile, saying, "I forgive you, my friend. I forgive you."

"At first I tried all the harder to break the prisoner's spirit as well as his body," Manuel confessed. "But instead *my* spirit began to change. Before long I couldn't face myself or face the love that came through his smile and words of forgiveness. *I* was the broken man. I left my country, and now I live here, trying to be of help to others."

Though the prisoner had been in a cell, he was the free man. No power on earth could control him. He could freely give up his life because he lived with a Christ-like love that could "endure the cross, despising the shame."

Martin Luther King Jr. described the nonviolent re- sisters of the civil-rights movement standing resolutely before snarling dogs, clubs, guns, and fire hoses. Cre- ative suffering empowers, he wrote, "because in its dominating spiritual quality it deprives the oppressor of the capacity to inflict harm. If harm is welcomed and is unopposed, it loses its power to create fear. Paradoxi- cally, the fear is then transferred to the aggressor, who has been deprived of his only strength—his capacity to evoke terror."

It is difficult to write about suffering. It seems ac- ademic if one has not felt the power that comes through creative suffering. I am certain, however, that this is what saints are made of. Thomas Merton stated, "No one can become holy without being plunged into the mystery of suffering, a mystery that is insoluble by an- alytical reasoning." To be holy is to be set aside, to be separated, different from the world and the world's un- derstanding of power. Suffering for the sake of a vision of the gospel, for the sake of enemy love is not reason- able, but with it comes a promise from Jesus: "Blessed are those who mourn, for they will be comforted. . . . Blessed are those who are persecuted because of righ- teousness, for theirs is the kingdom of heaven" (Matt. 5:4, 10).

Faithful lovers

We take a vow of nonviolence that includes possible suffering, not because we seek out suffering or allow ourselves to be victimized, but because we refuse to let the fear of suffering keep us from faithfulness. A com- mitment to love as Jesus loved may take us where we don't expect to go.

Visiting the mission fields in Africa several years ago, I realized how many missionary families have put themselves in situations where disease, lack of good diagnostic and medical resources, poor prenatal care, and scarcity of clean water contribute to poor health and even death. These missionaries have chosen to identify with the poor and, as the vow states, are "willing to enter into the suffering of others."

One spring we were in Cameroun visiting a young friend, Karen Bustad. Karen delighted in her work as a volunteer teacher in an African school. That summer Karen died of some mysterious illness. At her memorial service her father said, "If we had not taught Karen to love Jesus, she would still be with us." But her parents *had* taught her to love Jesus and to follow where she felt called to be.

Central to the nonviolence of Dr. Martin Luther King Jr. was faithfulness to love enemies regardless of the danger of personal suffering. Dr. King and his followers entered into the struggle of all blacks whose human rights were violated. He wrote:

> To our most bitter opponents we say: "We shall match your capacity to inflict suffering by our capacity to endure suffering. We shall meet your physical force with soul force. Do to us what you will, and we shall continue to love you. We cannot in all good conscience obey your unjust laws, because noncooperation with evil is as much a moral obligation as is cooperation with good . . . be ye assured that we will wear you down by our capacity to suffer. One day we shall win freedom, but not only for ourselves. We shall so appeal to your heart and conscience that we shall win you in the process, and our victory will be a double victory." (Quoted by Walter Wink, "The Transforming Power of Nonviolence," *Sojourners*, Feb. 1987.)

The blacks struggling for their civil rights were threatened, thrown in jail, hosed down with water. They were beaten and humiliated. Their homes were bombed. Though they were often terrified, they did not let the fear of suffering take away their trust in the power of nonviolent love. Like Gandhi's soul power *(satyagraha)* this love of enemies, indeed the suffering itself, had the power to change individuals and the conscience of a nation.

Our world is full of faithful lovers who understand the word *compassion*. The Latin roots of this word mean "to suffer with." Our willingness to do this is the result of putting our lives in the center of God's will. The apostle Paul's suffering for the sake of the gospel is well documented. He wrote to the Corinthian church that while we live in earthly tents, we sigh with anxiety. We groan and long to have God replace these tents with buildings provided by God (2 Cor. 5:1-4). Paul goes on to "boast" of his sufferings: "That is why, for Christ's sake, I delight in weaknesses, in insults, in hardships, in persecutions, in difficulties. For when I am weak, then I am strong" (2 Cor. 12:10). How could Paul feel this way? Because our faithful God said to Paul, and says to us, "My grace is sufficient for you, for my power is made perfect in weakness" (2 Cor. 12:9).

Fear is normal, but when we react out of our fear, we rarely have the good of our enemy in our heart. We are concerned only for our own safety. Fear becomes an adversary and makes us impotent. We relinquish the God-given power to change the anger and hostility out of which our opponent is acting. As someone said, "Perfect fear casts out love." I know this is true. Fear has the ability to keep us centered on self and prevents the risk that is necessary to change a violent situation.

Risk and the possibility of suffering have always gone hand in hand, but often this is forgotten when we speak of nonviolence. "But we might get hurt. What if nonviolence doesn't work?" When a young person goes to sign up for military service, the recruiter never says, "Good to have you with us. You can be assured you will not be hurt in the line of duty." Just the opposite is true. These young men and women assume that if they fulfill their role as soldiers, there is a strong possibility that they may suffer injury or even death. The same is true for the followers of gospel nonviolence. The risk comes with the job.

A newspaper reports that two firemen went into a building to save three young children. When they entered the smoke-filled house, they apparently thought little of their own safety. The firemen were heroes. They risked their lives to do their job. We honor our public servants and appreciate their concern for others, just as we in America have learned to honor our war heroes.

As Christians we also have a vocation. We have the gospel call to respond in love to those who want to harm us. This does not mean we won't have to suffer. If suffering occurs, it will be the result of our following the way of the cross.

"God has promised to make better lovers of us," says James Nelson. When God gives us the grace to desire and offer this extravagant love, God will also give us the grace to fulfill our vow. God does not abandon us, but suffers with us.

At a joyous celebration in a small village people dressed in costumes watched a parade, complete with jugglers and clowns. The children were flying kites, and somehow one little boy tore his kite.

"I will take this to the clown," the boy told his father.

"But the clown can't fix your kite, son," the parent replied.

"I know, but he can be sad with me," answered the child.

God is sad with us. That is why Jesus came, not to take our pain away, but to be part of our human condition, which includes suffering. Our God is a compassionate God, one who suffers with us, whether we be the poor and oppressed of the world, the abused child or spouse, or ordinary people who willingly put our lives alongside those who suffer to bring about a more just society.

In all the cross-shaped events of our lives, the power of God sustains us.

God, I trust in your sustaining love and believe that just as you gave me the grace and desire to offer this, so you will also bestow abundant grace to fulfill it.

ALL OF US CAN DO SOMETHING

Never doubt that a small group of thoughtful committed citizens can change the world; indeed, it's the only thing that ever has.

Margaret Mead

As I live with the vow of nonviolence, I am more and more grateful that it ends with a prayer. On those days when nonviolence seems impossible in a hardened world such as ours, I acknowledge by this prayer that I live by the grace of God. Extravagant love is a gift.

To live in a hardened world, to live with hardness of heart, is to live without hope. Hopelessness, despair, and apathy are sin. When the prophets and Jesus spoke of hearts that were hard, they were talking about people who no longer thought God was in control. These people thought they knew a better way to live, and they took the outcome of history into their own hands by acting unilaterally.

When evil seems to prevail and when things seem hopeless, we are tempted to respond to violence with "justified" violence. But to let go of nonviolent love, to let go of hope, is to be a coconspirator with evil. We play into the hands of the principalities and powers that rage through our world and play out their stories on the pages of our newspapers and on our television screens.

In one period of several weeks numerous people who have ample reason to be without hope touched my

life: a friend who is a victim of emotional violence, two
Central American refugees fleeing for their lives, the
unemployed who eat at the shelter where the Community of St. Martin serves meals, and a person be-
trayed by a close friend.

I was also privileged to visit with Lutheran Bishop
Kleopus Dumani from Namibia. We talked about hope.
I asked the question that many people ask the bishop:
"Do you have any hope for the situation in Namibia?"

He smiled and said, "Oh yes. I have hope, because
God will not abandon us. I have hope, because I continue to meet people all over the world who are concerned and who pray for us. I have hope, because injustice will never prevail. God is in charge."

To have hope is to trust that God's way of loving
and responding to violence is still the most powerful
force in the world. I believe that as God gives us the
desire to live with the gospel alternative to violence, so
God will give us grace to fulfill such a desire.

One person with God

On the tombstone of theologian John Knox are the
words, "One person with God is a majority." The words
speak of the hope of this man who struggled to be a
reformer of the church in the 16th century.

Take a critical look at the following statements.

LOIS: "There is nothing I as an individual can do to
make any difference." Having made such a statement
Lois can abandon any responsibility.

JIM: "I couldn't care less!" Jim's apathy is all he needs
to ignore any reconciliation in his life.

FRANCES: "I've got my future to think of. I'm so busy,
how can I work on reconciling a violent world?"

CHARLES: "Things have gotten past the point of no
return. We can't stop the process of the arms buildup."

CAROLYN: "It's all up to God." She is religious, but this pious statement is suspect if she means that God is to perform some sort of magic whereby human beings are not involved in creating *shalom*. Discipleship is to follow into those areas where God is working, not to take the outcome of the world into our own hands, reacting to our fears and violently imposing our will.

If I were an artist, I'd paint a vivid, splashy canvas of Isaiah's vision (Isaiah 6). Picture the drama of the prophet seeing God sitting high up on a throne. A seraph calls, "Holy, holy, holy! The whole earth is full of the glory of God!" And then the temple shakes and fills with smoke. Isaiah, in awe of such splendor, confesses that he is a person of unclean lips and lives in the midst of a people of unclean lips.

At this outpouring of his sinful condition and that of his world, a seraph takes a glowing coal from the altar and touches Isaiah's mouth with the words, "This coal has touched your lips, your guilt is taken away and your sin forgiven."

Then the voice of God calls out, "Whom shall I send? And who will go for us?"

Because repentance and forgiveness always lead to action on the part of the believer, Isaiah responds, "Here am I. Send me."

And God did send Isaiah. God sent Isaiah to speak to the people about their hardness of heart and about eyes that do not see.

Isaiah, a forgiven person, one person with God, was a majority. The world needs a critical mass of people who see reconciliation as an alternative to violence, but this critical mass begins with one person who is willing to act nonviolently on his or her convictions, one person who sees that injustice and violence are against the *sha-*

lom of God, one person who will say, "Here am I, God. Send me."

Because our world is nearly hardened, we seem to find little support for our values, but one person living differently from the rest of society can make a difference. Pascal wrote:

> When we are seated in a moving vessel and our eyes are fixed upon an object on the same vessel, we do not notice that we are moving. But if we look further, upon something that is not moving along with us, for instance upon the coast, we notice immediately that we are moving.
>
> It is the same with life. When the whole world lives wrongly, we fail to notice it, but should only one person awaken spiritually, the life of all others becomes immediately apparent. And the others always persecute those who do not live like them.

Followers of the nonviolent love of Jesus are not surprised that suffering may result from a counterculture life. Witness is always costly. Like grace, witness has never been cheap. Daniel Berrigan wrote that if we do not have peace, it is because we do not have peacemakers, and the reason there are no peacemakers "is because the making of peace is at least as costly as the making of war . . . at least as disruptive, at least as likely to bring disgrace" (*No Bars to Manhood*, 1970).

Hope-filled people transform their concern and their raw emotions into disciplined action for the sake of the people who suffer systematic and personal violence. It can begin with a simple act like that of Rosa Parks, who, fed up with having to sit in the back of the bus because of her color, refused to walk one more time past the empty front seats. With this solitary act of protest, the black civil-rights movement began to be organized.

All great social change begins because a few people committed to change take their anger and fear and outrage and begin to channel these emotions in a new way. One or two people refuse to be imprisoned by the status quo. One or two refuse to remain lukewarm and begin to tell one or two others of their concern.

Everett Rogers, a professor at the University of California in Berkeley, has studied how policies change and how social reform happens. Studying such events as the Vietnam war era and the civil rights movement, he discovered that for anything to happen, 50% of the population needs to be aware of the policy. When 5% of the people begin to speak out and to act, the policy is in trouble. When 20% of the awakened populace begins to speak out, the policy has very little chance of continuing.

In my own faith community, since Dan awakened us to the suffering of the people in Central America through his personal sharing and weeks of study, nearly half of us have been to El Salvador and Nicaragua.

Ann's deep concern resulted in organizing a vigil each week in the office of one of our senators to protest his voting record on Central America. Each Tuesday afternoon a small group presents a letter they have written to a member of the senator's staff. Articles from human rights organizations are included to substantiate the concerns of the letter. The discussion with the staff members ends with 10 minutes of silent prayer.

For two years the senator's staff graciously received members of the Community of St. Martin into their office. As a result of this nonviolent, respectful gathering, our senator has met personally with us on two occasions. He has even joined in prayer during vigils in his office. After more than two years he told the group that what they were doing had not gone unnoticed. "Your nonviolent vigils are known way beyond the walls of this office," he told Ann. "I appreciate your concern about the situation in Nicaragua, and I appreciate your prayers."

Partly because of our persistent peacemaking and that of other Minnesota groups concerned about our policies in Central America, the senator changed his vote in Congress and has joined us in our conviction that the continuation of arms to any faction of a government can only prolong the unrest, pain, and oppression we saw in Central America.

I would have been satisfied with visiting one senator, but not Ann. Six months ago she asked if anyone would vigil with her in the office of our other senator. I for one was very skeptical.

"Forget it, Ann. That senator's convictions and support of U.S. policy is too deeply entrenched. You're wasting your time. Count me out," I said.

Those hopeless words come back to haunt me as I see the relationship Ann and several others have been building with the senator and his staff. We considered it a minor miracle when Ann told us the senator had asked her and several other members of our community to have dinner with him to discuss their trip to Nicaragua and El Salvador and voice their concerns. Unlike me, Ann was more concerned with faithfully taking a stance than worrying whether her efforts would be successful.

Jesus told of a woman who wanted a hearing before the judge and said that because of her persistence the judge finally agreed to hear her problem. Jesus told this parable to teach us that we were "always to pray and not lose heart" (Luke 18:1 RSV). When I hear this parable, I think of Ann. She is an example to me of what it means not to lose heart but to pick up a piece of an injustice that needs to be held before us.

In his homily the day he was assassinated, Archbishop Oscar Romero of San Salvador said, "All of us can do something." Ann believes this. For her it is costly in terms of time and inconvenience, but no one said peacemaking was cheap.

All of us can do something. A mother took her small son for a walk each day in the park. She always carried with her a large, empty bag. "We can't pick up all the trash," she told her son, "but we can learn to pick up the trash directly in our path."

This is how we begin our peacemaking, by focusing on the injustice and the wrong we see immediately around us. It is not possible for us to pay attention to all the hurt and pain in the world, but if we open our eyes and each learns to "pick up the trash" in front of us, the world, as well as the environment, would be more peace-filled.

Help from the Spirit

Martin Luther's great song of faith, "A Mighty Fortress Is Our God," was written more than 400 years ago, but it is very contemporary.

> Though hordes of devils fill the land
> All threat'ning to devour us,
> We tremble not,
> unmoved we stand;
> They cannot overpow'r us.
> Let this the world's tyrant rage;
> In battle we'll engage!
> His might is doomed to fail;
> God's judgment must prevail!
> One little word subdues him.
>
> LBW 229

One little word? Can we trust that one word of God to bring peace and to conquer evil? That word is love. That word is Jesus. That word is forgiveness. Can a mustard seed faith in the word sustain us in this violent world?

"We tremble not, unmoved we stand," the hymn declares. I wish I could say that. But I confess that I am afraid—afraid of others, afraid of new ideas, of what might happen to my world, to my life-style, to my life. Luther believed that God would fight by our side, but the weapons of God's Spirit seem so inadequate next to the weapons of the world: MIRVS, MARVS, ICBM'S, SS 18s, 19s, 20s, the MX, Bison bombers, and Trident submarines. God's divine disarmament plan sounds strange to our ears because the weapons of the Spirit are gentleness, faithfulness, love, patience, forgiveness, truth, justice, and prayer.

Luther had the faith to sing:

> Were they to take our house,
> Goods, honor, child, or spouse,
> Though life be wrenched away,
> They cannot win the day.
> The Kingdom's ours forever!
>
> *LBW* 229

The kingdom is now, and the kingdom is to come. God is working in and around us. Many people who followed Jesus turned back because his way seemed difficult and impractical, and his sayings were too hard. But some, when asked by Jesus if they were not also going to leave, made a powerful statement of faith: "Lord, to whom shall we go? You have the words of eternal life" (John 6:68).

Our God is a great God. Throughout history people have continued to trust that we will be granted abundant grace to live according to God's will, relying on the weapons of the Spirit to bring peace to our lives, our communities, and our world. Hope is not so hard to find. We can risk extravagant love because God's grace sustains us.

> But this I call to mind and therefore I have hope: the steadfast love of the Lord never ceases, God's mercies never come to an end. They are new every morning; great is your faithfulness. "The Lord is my portion," says my soul, "therefore I will hope in God."
>
> (Lam. 3:21-24 author's paraphrase)